W9-BTZ-518

FOUR THINGS WOMEN WANT FROM A MAN

A. R. BERNARD

HOWARD BOOKS
AN IMPRINT OF SIMON & SCHUSTER, INC.

NEW YORK   NASHVILLE   LONDON   TORONTO   SYDNEY   NEW DELHI

Howard Books
An Imprint of Simon & Schuster, Inc.
1230 Avenue of the Americas
New York, NY 10020

Copyright © 2016 by A. R. Bernard

THE HOLY BIBLE, NEW INTERNATIONAL VERSION®, NIV® Copyright © 1973, 1978, 1984, 2011 by Biblica, Inc.® Used by permission. All rights reserved worldwide.

Scripture taken from the New King James Version®. Copyright © 1982 by Thomas Nelson. Used by permission. All rights reserved.

The Living Bible copyright © 1971 by Tyndale House Foundation. Used by permission of Tyndale House Publishers Inc., Carol Stream, Illinois 60188. All rights reserved. The Living Bible, TLB, and the The Living Bible logo are registered trademarks of Tyndale House Publishers.

Scripture quotations marked (NLT) are taken from the Holy Bible, New Living Translation, copyright © 1996, 2004, 2007 by Tyndale House Foundation. Used by permission of Tyndale House Publishers, Inc., Carol Stream, Illinois 60188. All rights reserved.

All rights reserved, including the right to reproduce this book or portions thereof in any form whatsoever. For information, address Howard Books Subsidiary Rights Department, 1230 Avenue of the Americas, New York, NY 10020.

First Howard Books trade paperback edition February 2017

HOWARD and colophon are trademarks of Simon & Schuster, Inc.

For information about special discounts for bulk purchases, please contact Simon & Schuster Special Sales at 1-866-506-1949 or business@simonandschuster.com.

The Simon & Schuster Speakers Bureau can bring authors to your live event. For more information or to book an event, contact the Simon & Schuster Speakers Bureau at 1-866-248-3049 or visit our website at www.simonspeakers.com.

Manufactured in the United States of America

10 9 8 7 6

Library of Congress Cataloging-in-Publication Data

Names: Bernard, A. R. (Alfonso R.) author.
Title: Four things women want from a man / A. R. Bernard.
Description: Nashville, TN : Howard Books, 2016.
Identifiers: LCCN 2016004123 | ISBN 9781501144653 (hardback)
Subjects: LCSH: Marriage. | Man-woman relationships. | Women—Psychology. |
   Men—Psychology. | BISAC: FAMILY & RELATIONSHIPS / Love & Romance. |
   FAMILY & RELATIONSHIPS / Marriage.
Classification: LCC HQ503 .B47 2016 | DDC 306.7—dc23 LC record available at
http://lccn.loc.gov/2016004123

ISBN 978-1-5011-4465-3
ISBN 978-1-5011-4671-8 (pbk)
ISBN 978-1-5011-4466-0 (ebook)

— CONTENTS —

— INTRODUCTION —

As the longtime pastor of a big-city church, I've had a front-row seat, a privileged place from which to observe the intimate details and the inner lives of New Yorkers from every walk of life. Along the way, I've witnessed almost every situation—and shared every emotion—in the dictionary: indescribable joys, unspeakable tragedies, and just about everything in between.

As men and women have come to me for spiritual counseling and practical advice over the years, I've identified familiar patterns of behavior that are repeated time and again. Although each person's situation is unique, the behaviors—and the consequences that result from them—are remarkably consistent. Now after almost four decades of preaching, teaching, and counseling, I've condensed my observations into this book, which offers a simple system for understanding the ways that couples relate to each other inside marriage—and outside it.

Why write this book now? Several reasons. The first reason has to do with men.

Being a responsible male in modern America is a full-time job, and a tough one at that. Never before in the history of humankind have distractions been so plentiful and temptations so prevalent. Even well intentioned men can become caught up in seemingly "harmless" behaviors that can quickly turn destructive. So I've written this book to provide an organized system of thought for men concerning women. By the time you are done with this book (or this book is done with you), a new vision of manhood will have emerged. You will understand and appreciate a woman's role in your life and how to bring out the best in every female relationship you might have. It will empower you to be a better husband for your wife, a better father for your daughter, a better brother for your sister, and so on. When a woman feels understood, it is easier for her to feel loved. When she feels loved, she is more inclined to give of herself in the relationship.

The second reason I wrote this book is that women need a better understanding of the qualities to look for in a man. Society tells us that fame, power, appearance, and money are all-important, so women today naturally seek these traits in a man. But looks can be deceiving, and, as the old saying goes, "All that glitters is not gold." On far too many occasions, I've seen women who thought their relationships were golden, only to find out later that they'd fallen for fool's gold instead of the real thing. Ladies, this book will change how you look at yourself and how you choose the man to whom you are willing to commit your life. It can save you the heartache of choosing the wrong man for the wrong reasons. You will be empowered to know what you want, want what you know, and not settle for less. You will engage in less experimentation with men and greater decisiveness in choosing the right man. By investing time thinking now about the qualities you want in a man, you can avoid relationship disasters that can wound your heart and spirit. And those of you already married can improve your relationship now by developing the traits outlined in this book.

A third reason I wrote this book has to do with the institution of marriage. In case you haven't noticed, marriage is under attack from all sides. It's my hope that this text can help couples navigate the stormy seas of modern matrimony by charting a course that's ultimately pleasing to the Ultimate Pilot.

Let me assure you this book is money and time well spent. Imagine if you had this information before that failed relationship. Well, it's time to get smart about relationships, BEFORE you get going. You have in these pages the four essential things women want/need in a healthy relationship with a man.

Enjoy!

— AUTHOR'S NOTE —
TO THE READER

This book is intended as a guide for both men and women. In certain passages, I've taken the liberty of speaking directly to men (in order to inform, encourage, motivate, and provide direction). In other passages, I address women (to help them better understand the men they love). Consequently, as you read through this book you will sometimes encounter directives that are obviously intended for the opposite sex. Please don't scan or skip these passages. Instead, read them carefully because they will, I trust, provide helpful insights.

In building better relationships, it's always worthwhile to see things from the other person's point of view.

By looking at things through your partner's eyes, you can gain empathy for—and a greater understanding of—the wants and needs of your mate. The more you understand about your loved one—and the more clearly you can see things from his or her point of view—the better your relationship will be.

So as you read the pages that follow, look carefully at the messages that are obviously intended for the opposite gender. These passages may contain nuggets of gold that you can use today, tomorrow, and for many years to come.

— AUTHOR'S NOTE ABOUT —
THE WOMEN QUOTED IN THIS TEXT

In preparation for this book, I spoke with and received written responses from a number of women from various backgrounds. I am, of course, extremely grateful to all those who offered their assistance, their advice, and their insights.

Below are brief biographical notes about each contributor. To preserve confidentiality, I have chosen to use only their first names and last initials.

Allison C.: Italian, age thirty-one, married three years.

Angie B.: Teacher, married eighteen years.

Gail M.: Author, international speaker, married eighteen years, currently living in South Africa.

Jackie P.: Successful CEO, mother.

Kerry B.: Owns a successful business and is a home-maker, age fifty-four, married twenty-seven years.

Ruthie S.: Scandinavian, lives in the Midwest, business owner and CFO, mother, wife.

Sally P.: Chinese, age fifty-two, married twenty-five years.

Vivian C.: The CEO of an international company, age fifty.

— 1 —

FOUR THINGS

A man without an organized system
of thought will always be at the
mercy of a man who has one.

—Edwin Louis Cole

You live in a complicated world, a world filled to the brim with temptations, distractions, disruptions, and diversions. Here in the twenty-first century, it's easier than ever to lose your way because there are so many ways to lose it. With so many outlets vying for your attention and your time, there's scarcely a spare moment to organize your thoughts and prioritize your life.

So, in the interest of making things as simple as possible, I'm going to give you an organized system of thought, a four-word formula that, if applied consistently, can help *any* man become a *better* man and a *better* husband.

If you're a man who genuinely wants to stay on the right path, nobody needs to tell you that there are countless opportunities to choose the wrong path. The devil, it seems, has a bigger toolkit than ever before, and he's not afraid to use it. So it's hard to be a godly guy in a temptation-filled world. Hard, but *not impossible*.

IN ORDER TO FIND THE RIGHT PATH AND STAY ON IT, THERE ARE FOUR THINGS GOD WANTS FROM YOU, FOUR CHARACTER TRAITS THAT CAN BRING PEACE TO YOUR HEART AND HAPPINESS TO YOUR HOME. THESE FOUR TRAITS, WHEN PRACTICED REGULARLY, HAVE THE POWER TO TRANSFORM BOYS (OF ANY AGE) INTO MEN.

To find the right path and stay on it, God wants four things from you, four character traits that can bring peace to your heart and happiness to your home. These four traits, when practiced regularly, have the power to transform boys (of any age) into men. But this book isn't only for men; it's also a book for the women who love them. So, if you're a woman who's trying to help your man reach his full potential, then you need to understand these four traits, too.

You can think of these four things as an organized way of thinking and behaving based on rock-solid principles that are as true today as they were at the dawn of time, because they were established by the Creator:

There are four things that God wants from a man: maturity, decisiveness, consistency, and strength.

There are four things that a woman wants from a man: maturity, decisiveness, consistency, and strength.

There are four things that a man struggles with in life: maturity, decisiveness, consistency, and strength.

And, there's an inherent tension between men and women that goes back to the Fall of Adam and Eve. That tension is based on a woman's need for maturity, decisiveness, consistency, and strength from a man.

On the pages that follow, I'll discuss these four essential key traits; I'll also explain why women want them and what men can do to develop them. But before we get started, let me share how I came to write this book. I suppose it began in 1953, in the country of my birth: Panama.

My mother, Adelina Bernard, was a Panamanian sprinter who qualified for but did not compete in the 1952 Olympics. When I was four years old, my mom moved us to Brooklyn, New York. I grew up in "the 'hood" without a father, and I spent much of my youth trying to resolve a crisis of identity.

I was searching for my own identity.

I was searching for male role models.

And I was searching for God.

From all my reading—and I read a lot—I concluded that God, truth, and reality were synonymous and that if I found one, the other two would be present.

In the 1960s, America was in great social, political, cultural, and spiritual transition. I was socially conscious at an early age; I spent my teen years looking for identity in social movements. Looking for Black Identity and social reform, I landed in the Nation of Islam. After five years of being fully engaged in the Nation of Islam, God seized my heart on January 11, 1975, while attending a meeting led by Nicky Cruz, former leader of the notorious Mau Mau street gang. On that night, something deep and profound happened inside of me. I heard an inner voice that carved two statements on my heart: "I'm the God you're looking for," and "I and my Word are one."

It was not the *institution* of Christianity that attracted me; it was the *person* of Jesus Christ.

This transformation God had on my heart changed me forever. The people in my life could tell something was different—especially one very special person. Karen and I had met in high school. She was the rule follower and I was the rebel. Thankfully, opposites did attract, and the bond of love created then has lasted almost forty years. Three months after I heard God's voice, Karen also gave her life to Christ, and we began studying God's Word together, a practice that continues today. We dated for three years and then married. That was forty-three years ago, during which time God has blessed us with seven sons and twenty-one grandchildren.

"They say opposites attract, and I know a couple who prove it's true. They are very different in many ways; however, their love for each other is so honest and pure that just being around them makes me smile. They were high school sweethearts who married young over forty years ago and have enjoyed triumphs, weathered storms, and remained true to God, true to themselves, and true to each other. It's like watching harmony in action."

—JACKIE P.

In 1978, Karen and I began a tiny ministry in our kitchen. The following year, I left a ten-year career in banking and entered the ministry full-time. Karen and I prayed constantly for our ministry, as did the small band of believers who composed our congregation. Those prayers must have worked because today our church, which sits on an eleven-and-a-half-acre campus in Brooklyn, has a registered membership of 37,000.

After thirty-seven years of teaching, preaching, and counseling in the heart of one of the world's most diverse cities, I've seen almost every kind of marital situation. I've seen blissfully happy couples, and I've seen profoundly sad ones. I've seen peaceful couples and belligerent couples. I've seen "perfect" marriages blow up overnight, and I've seen rocky relationships repaired overnight, too.

Along the way, I've come to understand the patterns and principles that, when applied day in and day out, make marriages work. I've also observed the patterns of behavior that are almost certain to destroy any loving relationship. This book will help readers recognize the good patterns and avoid the bad ones.

The Scripture 1 Peter 3:7 teaches husbands to "treat your wife with understanding," (NLT), but most men don't do this naturally. Most men simply aren't hard-wired to be keen observers of their wives; they often miss obvious signs that could have helped them avoid headaches and heartbreaks had those warnings been heeded early on. So, I've written this book for men to help them better understand themselves *and* their wives.

Women, on the other hand, are *very* keen observers. They understand their husbands' patterns; they understand the ways their men are likely to behave in any given situation. Wives know their husbands better than anyone—other than God, of course—does. But often, women don't understand *themselves* as well as they understand their men. So I've also written this book for women, to help them understand *themselves* better, understand *their men* better, and understand *their marriages* better.

SO I'VE ALSO WRITTEN THIS BOOK FOR WOMEN, TO HELP THEM UNDERSTAND *THEMSELVES* BETTER, UNDERSTAND *THEIR MEN* BETTER, AND UNDERSTAND *THEIR MARRIAGES* BETTER.

Women dream of men in the ideal but marry the real.

—EDWIN LOUIS COLE

After almost four decades as a pastor and counselor, I've learned that the old adage "There's nothing new under the sun" applies to men, women, and relationships. The way Adam related to Eve—and vice versa—has much to teach us about the way men and women interact today.

Adam was employed (by God) before he was married. And so it was that the very first man had the very first job: Adam tended God's garden (Genesis 2:15).

As a working man with few distractions, Adam obviously took his career seriously. In time, God entrusted him with a second job: naming the animals. Picture Adam putting in long hours in the Garden of Eden, and working two jobs with no woman in sight. No wonder he became focused on his career!

Since Adam had his work *before* he had his wife, he was a man on a mission. It's no surprise then that men today still tend to identify themselves with their work. And it shouldn't be shocking to any of us that guys are still "mission minded."

There was a time in my life, marriage, and ministry when I was guilty of the sin of transposition. My priorities were seriously out of order. It was 1984 and almost the end of my marriage. The problem was simply found in my priorities, or wrong priorities: ministry (career) first, then people, then my family.

It led to the greatest stress Karen and I have ever experienced. She miscarried a set of twins, I withdrew, and the distance between us became very great. Karen will tell you that her heart became bitter toward me and her competition: the ministry. A man's wife should never have to compete with his career for his time and affection. But at the time, I was a man on a mission, sanctioned by God. Everyone had to understand, especially my wife and children. But what I failed to see then was that they were the test of my ministry. If I couldn't pastor my home by being a good leader, husband, and father, how could I pastor a congregation? It actually took a year for me to sort this out.

By March 1985, I found myself in a hotel room in Dallas, Texas, waiting to attend a pastors' conference at Prestonwood Baptist Church. In a moment of time, I felt the full weight of responsibility for the condition of my marriage land on my shoulders. After wiping away the tears, I called Karen and asked her forgiveness. I explained that I was fully responsible for the condition of things between us. The hurt and bitterness in her shrugged off my apologies. But it didn't matter; I needed this change, regardless of her acceptance of its legitimacy. This was one of those inner-voice moments: "Deepen your relationship with your wife, and I'll broaden your ministry."

It was there that I began my journey to understand her role in my life and work. She was my support system, my accountability factor, and my "personal brand" protector! I was stifling her greatest value to me! She needed to know that I valued her and her input in my life and work. I needed to affirm her role. It took a crisis, but I got it. Did she forgive me? Well, that was a process, and a lot took place during the process. The details are revolutionary, but we'll discuss them in the next chapter.

———◄O►———

God created Eve to help Adam (Genesis 2:18). Today, women still desperately want to help their men. But men, being mission minded to the point of stubbornness, often misinterpret their wives' efforts. What the woman believes to be much-need assistance, the man perceives to be much-dreaded nagging. And when the wires of marital communication get crossed, it's only a matter of time until sparks begin to fly—and not the good kind, either.

> WHAT THE WOMAN BELIEVES TO BE MUCH-NEED ASSISTANCE, THE MAN PERCEIVES TO BE MUCH-DREADED NAGGING.

So what's the solution? I'm glad you asked. The solution comes when both husbands and wives gain a better understanding of the values, the patterns, and the principles that form the basis for a successful marriage. The solution comes when couples employ an organized system that guides their words, thoughts, motives, actions, and attitudes. And the solution comes when men exhibit four traits that are pleasing to God as well as to their wives.

Perhaps you're a married person who wants to improve your communication at home. Or maybe you're a single person who's thinking seriously about marriage. Or perhaps you're simply an inquisitive single who wants to learn more about the institution of marriage. Whatever your status, the concepts on these pages have the power to transform your life. And I pray that they will. I've seen them work in many others' hearts.

So, with no further delay, join me as we take a closer look at the culture of marriage.

— QUESTIONS FOR REFLECTION —

Before starting this journey, think about the importance of the four traits in your own life. Do you agree that these are the four essential traits? Is there a trait you'd add or replace? What are you first thoughts on this experience?

_____

_____

_____

_____

_____

_____

_____

_____

_____

_____

_____

_____

_____

_____

_____

_____

_____

_____

_____

_____

_____

_____

_____

_____

_____

_____

_____

_____

MEN: What trait seems the hardest to develop? Which one looks easiest for you?

WOMEN: What trait do you appreciate the most in a partner? Which have you valued the least?

_____

_____

_____

_____

_____

_____

_____

_____

_____

_____

_____

_____

_____

_____

_____

_____

_____

_____

_____

_____

_____

_____

_____

_____

_____

_____

_____

_____

_____

_____

— PRAYER —

FOR MEN: Dear God, as I begin this journey to develop these four traits, I ask that you keep my heart and mind open and allow me to embrace this process fully. I want to be a better man and a better partner. Lord, help me to be willing to embrace change and grow closer to You. In Your name I pray, Amen.

FOR WOMEN: Dear God, please be with my partner as he embarks on this journey. I want to be the best support I can be for him. Open my heart and mind to your will. In Your name I pray, Amen.

— 2 —

THE CULTURE
OF MARRIAGE,
THEN AND NOW

"Define yourself radically as one
beloved by God. This is the true self.
Every other identity is illusion."

—Brennan Manning, *Abba's Child*

We tend to think of marriage as a static, unchanging institution. But it's not. Throughout history, the roles played by husbands and by wives have been transformed. And so have their expectations.

Your ancestors had a very different view of marriage than you do. The same culture that shaped their world also shaped the way they structured their relationships. They lived in a different time; they survived in a different society; they built their families according to different norms; they lived, loved, worked, and died in a culture you might scarcely recognize.

Culture is that integrated system of beliefs, traditions, customs, values, products, technologies, and ideas that constitute the life of a people. Culture is humanity's way of making sense of the world around us; it is our way of determining the most efficient and effective strategies for dealing with our own reality, our own particular circumstances, our past, our present, and our future.

Cultures are formed by mankind's response to basic needs; the more creative the response, the more advanced the culture. Today, as we look around the world, we see the stark contrast between advanced cultures—where basic needs are almost always met—and third world societies where even elemental needs such as food and shelter often go unmet. The gap between the haves and the have-nots is vast, and so are the ways that they must approach their daily lives.

Some cultures are broad and diverse, like mine. I live in New York City. My hometown has cultures within cultures. On one block, you may encounter a distinct ethnic tradition; walk around the corner, and you'll find a completely different vibe, with different customs, traditions, mores, and styles. It's what former mayor David Dinkins called "the mosaic of New York."

In other places, cultures are more homogenous: people tend to think alike, dress alike, and behave alike. Their collective realities are shaped not by variety, but by consistency of thought and action. Yet even in these homogeneous societies, customs evolve. In today's world, the pace of cultural evolution is quickening, and there's no indication that things will slow down anytime soon.

When any culture begins to redefine itself, people feel adrift. In the 1970 bestseller *Future Shock*, Alvin Toffler described the confusion that results when traditional values are in flux. He called this phenomenon "rootlessness." What was true for Toffler forty years ago is just as true today. As societal norms change at an ever quickening pace, both men and women may feel

> AS SOCIETAL NORMS CHANGE AT AN EVER QUICKENING PACE, BOTH MEN AND WOMEN MAY FEEL UPROOTED, CONFUSED, AND DISORIENTED.

uprooted, confused, and disoriented. It is within this context that the relationships between husbands and wives are being redefined by popular culture.

What was considered extreme fifty years ago may be considered normal today. What was considered outlandish—or even illegal—then, may be considered quite ordinary now. Don't believe me? Turn on your radio or TV. Pop culture reinforces the new rules and sends out messages that describe a "new normal": the latest fad, whatever it happens to be. Then pop culture tries to convince us that the new norm is the solution to all our troubles.

WHAT WAS CONSIDERED EXTREME FIFTY YEARS AGO MAY BE CONSIDERED NORMAL TODAY. WHAT WAS CONSIDERED OUTLANDISH— OR EVEN ILLEGAL—THEN, MAY BE CONSIDERED QUITE ORDINARY NOW.

But there's a problem: although culture undergoes constant change, the hearts and minds of men and women are not nearly so malleable. Societal values change, the world changes, and our culture is transformed day by day. But our hearts and minds, which were engineered by a Higher Power, are not so readily altered. Like it or not, our hearts and minds have been hardwired. Society can change the programming and even install a new operating system, but we can't change the circuitry that we're born with.

Even if the culture says, "Don't worry; you can do this, or you can do that," new norms are doomed to fail if they aren't congruent with our internal sense of right and wrong. The world can tell us "It's okay," but if our conscience disagrees, society's "new" value system will self-destruct along with the people who have embraced it.

> NEW NORMS ARE DOOMED TO FAIL IF THEY AREN'T CONGRUENT WITH OUR INTERNAL SENSE OF RIGHT AND WRONG.

Historian Stephanie Coontz and sociologist Andrew J. Cherlin have written extensively on the topics of marriage and divorce. They've attempted to answer an important question: why are we, as a society, marrying less and divorcing more? It's a simple question with a very complicated answer, but the CliffsNotes version is this: our twenty-first-century attitudes toward marriage and divorce have changed because our nation's culture has changed. The transformation has been remarkable.

America began as an agrarian economy. Most families lived in small farming communities, far from the big cities. These folks earned their living from the land. Families were large because children were expected to work in the fields. Without large institutions or mass media, parents assumed almost total responsibility for educating and acculturating their children. Values were taught in the home; etiquette, religion, and conduct were handed down from grandparent to parent, from parent to child. Coontz and Cherlin call this "the era of institutional marriage," and it lasted from the founding of America until the middle of the nineteenth century.

During this era, marriage was considered as an essential institution. Divorce was almost unheard of.

A century ago man's chief concern was his spiritual life; now his chief concern is with his physical and temporal affairs.

—BILLY GRAHAM

In those days, people approached marriage differently. If they fell in love with their spouse, that was undeniably a good thing. But it was not the *primary* thing. People didn't marry for love. If you were a man, you married because it was the accepted way to live with the woman who would bear your children. If you were a woman, you married for provision, for shelter, and for protection from the violent realities of life on the frontier. For married couples, strong emotional connections, while desirable, were not essential.

Then, the culture began to change.

From 1850 until the middle of the next century, Americans experienced an industrial revolution. People began moving to the cities, where they found better-paying jobs. During these years, women earned the right to vote and the right to join the workforce. They also earned the right to attend institutions of higher learning. Children were increasingly socialized in big-city neighborhoods and in public schools, not at home or on the farm.

With their newfound freedoms, marriageable women began to expect different things from prospective husbands. Marriage became a search, not only for protection and provision, but also for affection and companionship. People viewed marriage as the way to find love and to experience sexual fulfillment. This period (1850–1955) is known as the time of "compassionate

> IT WAS A TIME WHEN COUPLES MARRIED FOR REASONS OF THE HEART, OFTEN TOSSING PRACTICALITIES ASIDE.

marriage." It was a time when couples married for reasons of the heart, often tossing practicalities aside. The compassionate model of marriage was reflected in the romantic movies of the post–World War II era: Boy met girl; boy and girl fell in love; boy and girl got married and lived happily ever after. Roll the credits.

Until the 1960s. That's when America experienced another revolution or, more accurately, a *series* of revolutions. Americans experienced a social revolution, a sexual revolution, a musical revolution, political revolutions, and religious revolutions, to name but a few. As these revolutions took hold, society's view of marriage evolved from the "compassionate" to the "self-expressive," which is where we are now as a society.

In the self-expressive marriage, spouses seek to discover who they "really" are. Each partner

> IN THE SELF-EXPRESSIVE MARRIAGE, SPOUSES SEEK TO DISCOVER WHO THEY "REALLY" ARE. EACH PARTNER IS ON A MISSION OF SELF-DEFINITION, A JOURNEY TOWARD SELF-ACTUALIZATION.

is on a mission of self-definition, a journey toward self-actualization. This means that more and more people are marrying, but not for provision, security, or even for love. People are searching for personal growth and individual satisfaction. This view of marriage is self-centered, which is one reason that our divorce rates are skyrocketing. The self-expressive marriage is "me based."

> MARRIAGE IS AN EMPATHETIC UNION, NOT A DISCOVERY OF ONE'S "TRUE SELF."

It doesn't work because marriage is not a "me-based" proposition. Marriage is an empathetic union, not a discovery of one's "true" self.

"I don't know how many times I've heard couples part ways saying, 'We have just grown apart,' or 'He doesn't meet my needs anymore.' I think the greatest threat to a marriage is selfishness. Being self-absorbed and self-centered is no way to build a team."

—JACKIE P.

The self-expressive marriage is a recipe for midlife crisis because it inevitably leads to a crisis of identity when wives or husbands convince themselves that self-actualization is more important than commitment. They believe (wrongly) that self-gratification is the goal. They seek *self*-satisfaction, not *mutual* satisfaction. And, if that weren't bad enough, both husbands and wives can be surprisingly impatient. They know what they want and when they want it: *now*.

This is the culture in which we live.

As a pastor and counselor, I often speak with couples who are trying to make sense of their relationships in a world where self-expressive connections are the norm. Sometimes these couples are married, trying to avoid divorce. On other occasions, I speak with men and women *before* they exchange their wedding vows. Although their particular circumstances vary widely, the underlying issues are remarkably similar. All too often, couples are focused on the wrong thing. They're

FOUR THINGS WOMEN WANT FROM A MAN

> ALL TOO OFTEN, COUPLES ARE FOCUSED ON THE WRONG THING. THEY'RE FOCUSED ON THEMSELVES AS *INDIVIDUALS*, NOT ON THEMSELVES AS PART OF AN *INDIVISIBLE* UNION.

focused on themselves as *individuals*, not on themselves as part of an *indivisible* union.

The very same culture that brought us Twitter feeds and selfies has encouraged us to value partying above responsibility, fun above maturity, self-expression above humility, and pleasure above commitment. Couples seem anxious to receive the benefits of a permanent relationship (happiness, security, love, sex, and companionship), but they're often unwilling to make the sacrifices required to reap those benefits. What's required, by the way, is total commitment, in good times and hard times. It's a price, unfortunately, that many couples simply aren't willing to pay.

Given the new cultural norms, it's no surprise that couples are waiting longer to get married. Even living together is becoming passé. The idea of committing oneself to another human being for an entire lifetime may seem too confining—too permanent. So we're staying single longer and divorcing more frequently than ever before. Cherlin describes this as the "de-institutionalization" of marriage, and it's redefining the way we think, the way we live, and the way we raise our children.

Marriage should be an empathetic union where the needs of one are felt by the other. But we've gotten away from that. Instead, modern culture has convinced us that our marriage partner should be the unofficial tour guide on our own personal journey of self-actualization. So here's what happens: a spouse cruises along for a decade or two, fulfilling all the

> MODERN CULTURE HAS CONVINCED US THAT OUR MARRIAGE PARTNER SHOULD BECOME THE UNOFFICIAL TOUR GUIDE ON OUR OWN PERSONAL JOURNEY OF SELF-ACTUALIZATION.

socially accepted obligations—earning a paycheck, raising the kids—expecting the "self-discovery part" of the marriage to begin any day. Then, one morning, the spouse wakes up, perhaps on the wrong side of the bed, and experiences an epiphany: time's running out! So the spouse announces, "I just realized that I haven't been realized!" In this fashion, the marital gauntlet is thrown down, and the midlife crisis begins.

So what are we to do? The answer lies not in pop-culture solutions, but in solutions we find in Paul's letter to the Ephesians. He wrote, "Husbands, love your wives, just as Christ loved the church and gave himself up for her" (5:25 NIV). Christ loved His church unconditionally and sacrificially. That's how men are instructed to love their wives. No exceptions.

SACRIFICIAL LOVE IS, BY DEFINITION, LONG-TERM LOVE. IT'S NOT ABOUT THE PLEASURE OF THE MOMENT; IT'S ABOUT CONSISTENT RESPECT, DAY AFTER DAY, YEAR AFTER YEAR.

Sacrificial love is, by definition, long-term love. It's not about the pleasure of the moment; it's about consistent respect, day after day, year after year. Sacrificial love requires generational thinking, which means that couples consider the impact of the success or failure of their relationship on the next generation. And it's about loving the other person, not just when it's easy, but also when it's hard.

In the last chapter, I shared with you my sin of transposition, having my priorities out of order. I began the process of change, but Karen offered her forgiveness on an installment basis. She watched for consistency and gradually began to forgive. She was treating forgiveness as a reward instead of as a gift that flows from the value you place on the relationship. What I didn't know until a few years later was that her resistance grew from a root of bitterness that had formed in her heart from all we had gone through.

It came to a head in 1994. Ten years had passed,

and our relationship had experienced dramatic change for the better. But at times we found ourselves arguing over the slightest thing. One morning in our new home, we got into this big argument about where to place the television in the kitchen. I know: ridiculous! Well, I thought so, but she was very serious. When the temperature hit the boiling point, I felt it was time for me to head to the office.

On my way, I prayed and asked God, "What am I missing?" A word of revelation hit my mind like a bolt of lightning. Bitterness! I began the process of self-examination. Was I bitter toward her? Was she bitter toward me? What is bitterness, really? I was compelled to share it with her, but I had to be wise. I found the text in Hebrews chapter 12, verse 15, "Looking carefully lest anyone fall short of the grace of God, lest any root of bitterness springing up cause trouble, and by this many become defiled." So I called her and shared the text with her, never mentioning the word *bitterness*. I apologized and said, "Let's talk about this when I get home." She agreed. The rest of the day was spent understanding this passage of Scriptural wisdom focusing on the word *bitterness*. I was amazed at what I found.

Bitterness must take root before it springs up! In other words, it festers in the heart and begins to manifest in your relationships. It stems from disappointments that accumulate over time but are not acknowledged or addressed. These disappointments result from expectations that were never met; whether they were reasonable or unreasonable doesn't matter. What matters most are the feelings of hurt and grief. Bitterness begins to color the lens through which we see and interpret the words, attitudes, and actions of the one we believe has hurt us. Even a loving "Good morning, dear" becomes suspect. The hurt begins to overshadow the relationship, creating an environment of tension that easily triggers a major argument from the slightest disagreement. This was the environment in which Karen and I lived. Now I had the words to explain it.

When I got home that evening, I waited until things settled down. Then I casually popped the question: "What did you get out of that verse?" She was hesitant at first, then she turned to me and said, "Bitterness." I was floored! This was the word! Karen proceeded to tell me that she had her own moment of repentance. She didn't want to believe that this was what was in her heart, but it was the word that stood out as she read the passage. She asked God to forgive her and to release her from this bitterness. She began her own journey of change and renewal. It was a liberating moment similar to my own ten years before. Imagine that something can be rooted in the heart and continue for years until it is discovered and rooted out. Forgiveness released both of us that day!

I share this story be-
cause I want you to
know, without a doubt,
that marriage is a work
in progress. If there are

IF THERE ARE THREE WORDS
THAT EXPRESS THE SECRET TO
LONGEVITY IN A RELATIONSHIP,
THEY MUST BE *ADAPT* AND *ADJUST*.

two words that express the secret to longevity in a relationship, they must be *adapt* and *adjust*. Adaptability is
having the knowledge and the willingness to accommo-
date new conditions. Growing relationships are always
facing new conditions that challenge the strength of the
union. Adaptability has to do with major changes. Ad-
justment, on the other hand, has to do with the slight
alterations, the small changes that are necessary for the
good of the relationship. Adapting and adjusting is a
never-ending process and the key to longevity.

God's objective for marriage is to model two inter-
related concepts that we have a problem with in this
society: love and commitment. We want to fall in love,
but we're unwilling to commit for the long term. We

want love without commitment. We want involve-
ment without commitment. We want the benefits of
marriage—sex, security, and children—without the sacrifice. So we put conditions on our spouse based on society's unrealistic expectations, and when those faulty expectations go unmet, we grumble or worse.

SO WE PUT CONDITIONS ON OUR
SPOUSE BASED ON SOCIETY'S
UNREALISTIC EXPECTATIONS, AND
WHEN THOSE FAULTY EXPECTATIONS
GO UNMET, WE GRUMBLE OR WORSE.

Our attention spans are short. We live in a world of text talk (LOL, OMG! BFF, L8R) where almost everything is condensed and distilled into brief, instantaneous bursts. So we've become short-term thinkers, seeking immediate rewards, avoiding long-term communications and long-term relationships of any kind. But that's not what marriage is about. Marriage is not a short-term proposition; it's not designed for instant gratification. It's about thinking generationally.

Modern culture tires to convince you that all the rules have changed, that God's model for marriage is no longer valid, and that the old system just doesn't work anymore. But the message of modern culture is untrue. The model for a successful marriage isn't out of date. In fact, the formula hasn't changed since the New Testament times when Jesus advised husbands and wives to become so totally committed to each other that "they are no longer two but one flesh" (Matthew 19:6 NKJV).

The Man from Galilee taught us that a successful marriage isn't about *selfishness*; it's about *selflessness*. It isn't about *finding yourself*; it's about *binding yourselves* to each other. When two people truly become one, that's the two-thousand-year-old formula that works. Anything less is a prescription for disaster, no matter what the culture says.

"If you don't grow together, you will grow apart." Growing apart is automatic. Growing together is a choice. That choice requires discipline and commitment.

We use a great book in our premarital program entitled *His Needs, Her Needs: Building an Affair-Proof Marriage*, by Willard F. Harley Jr. I recommend it highly to couples getting married or having trouble in their marriage. All relationships are based on needs. Harley covers the basic needs of each partner in the marriage relationship. When we focus on each other's needs as well as our own, it protects us from selfishness. Selfishness is a sign of immaturity, which is a failure to accept responsibility for anyone other than one's self. This is why I call marriage an empathetic union. Empathy is my willingness to open myself up to the feelings and needs of the one I love and make them my own!

———◀◦▶———

On the pages that follow, I'll examine the institution of marriage, not as defined by pop culture or social norms, but as defined by God. His formula hasn't changed, it's not going to change, and it doesn't need to change—because it works. Always has. Always will.

It's a formula based on proven patterns and eternal principles.

— QUESTIONS FOR REFLECTION —

When you think about the changes the institution of marriage has gone through, how do you feel? How have you or your partner let self-expression get in the way of commitment? How have you had to adapt and adjust in your own relationship? Have you seen bitterness take root in your own life? How have you dealt with it?

_____

_____

_____

_____

_____

_____

_____

_____

_____

_____

_____

_____

_____

_____

_____

_____

_____

_____

_____

_____

_____

_____

_____

_____

_____

_____

_____

— PRAYER —

FOR MEN: God, I believe you created marriage, and I want to honor that creation. Show me ways in which I have put self-actualization ahead of Your will. Help me to adapt and adjust. I want to let go of "finding myself" and instead "bind myself" to my spouse. In Your name, Amen.

FOR WOMEN: Lord, please help me make the necessary sacrifices, along with my spouse, so that my marriage will be centered on an indivisible union instead of an individual. In Your name I pray, Amen.

— 3 —

PATTERNS AND PRINCIPLES

**We must adjust to changing times and
still hold to unchanging principles.**

—Jimmy Carter

The book of Genesis describes patterns of character and behavior that have come to *all* men and women from the *original* man and woman. This historical record affords us the opportunity to understand God's plan for marriage. If we acknowledge His patterns and use them as the cornerstone of our relationships, we are inevitably blessed. But Genesis also serves as a clear warning to those who would ignore God's guidance.

COUPLES WHO CHOOSE TO DISREGARD GOD'S BLUEPRINT FOR MARRIAGE DO SO AT THEIR OWN RISK.

Couples who choose to disregard God's blueprint for marriage do so at their own risk.

"I know that God has a plan for our marriage. Some days, it's easy to understand that plan, and some days it's harder. That's why we must ask for God's guidance every day."

—ANGIE B.

Here Angie raises the question, how does God guide us on a daily basis? We understand the wisdom and guidance that comes from the study of Scripture. But a wonderful passage of Scripture speaks to this daily guidance. It is found in the Psalms of David 37:23. The translation that expresses the beauty of the text is the New Living Translation. It reads, "The Lord directs the steps of the godly. He delights in every detail of their lives." First, it's exciting to know that although God is

ALTHOUGH GOD IS INVOLVED IN WORLD AFFAIRS AND RUNNING THIS VAST UNIVERSE IN WHICH WE LIVE, HE STILL CARES ABOUT THE DETAILS OF OUR LIVES.

involved in world affairs and running this vast universe in which we live, he still cares about the details of our lives. The key word in the text is *direct*. How does God direct?

The word *direct* means to cause someone's attention, thoughts, or emotions to relate to a particular person, thing, cause, goal, or objective. God knows how to draw our attention and how to influence our thoughts and emotions in ways that move in a certain direction. I cannot tell you how many times I have felt a divine hand at work in my life, opening doors and bringing the right people into my life. God has a plan for you and your relationships!

———◇———

God designed men and women according to a perfect plan: *His* plan. Trusting that plan is essential if we are to build better relationships, better marriages, and happier homes. But increasingly, it seems that happy homes are getting harder to find. Traditional values are being *de*-valued by modern culture, and marriage is under attack.

During the twentieth century, women gained rights in the workplace, in the voting booth, and in our institutions of higher learning—all good things. Thankfully, the trend continues. It's been a long struggle, and the struggle isn't over. But here in the twenty-first century, women are increasingly evaluated, not by gender stereotypes, but by their abilities and their contributions. These changes, long overdue, have done much to level the professional playing fields and to bring fairness into everyday American life. As a nation, we're improving slowly—far too slowly at times—but surely. As Dr. Martin Luther King, Jr. correctly observed, "The arc of the moral universe is long, but it bends toward justice."

While the benefits of the women's rights movement and the continued efforts for equality have made our country a far better place, there has been an unintended consequence: As a society, we've managed to confuse equal *rights* with equal *roles*. We've

> AS A SOCIETY, WE'VE MANAGED TO CONFUSE EQUAL *RIGHTS* WITH EQUAL *ROLES*.

come to believe, wrongly, that the roles of husband and wife are interchangeable. Guided by this mistaken notion, we've arrived at an erroneous conclusion: that role reversal inside the marriage is not only an acceptable thing but also a desirable thing. We've confused equal treatment *under the law* with equal roles *inside the marriage.*

> WE'VE CONFUSED EQUAL TREATMENT *UNDER THE LAW* WITH EQUAL ROLES *INSIDE THE MARRIAGE.*

Let me take a moment to make an observation that is so obvious, so easily recognized, so completely, totally, and indisputably apparent that it *almost* doesn't need to be stated. But I'll state it anyway: *men and women are different.*

Very different.

Not just *physically* different.

Not just *emotionally* different.

Not just *psychologically* different.

Men and women are different in all these ways and more. But modern culture has encouraged us to ignore these differences, with the predictably poor consequences. Husbands and wives have become confused about the roles they're expected to play inside a "modern" relationship. Yet the internal constructs of human nature are not in flux. They were established by our Creator long ago. And, like every other thing that God created, He did it according to His own principles and patterns, irrespective of cultural trends.

So it's time to rethink the institution of marriage, not based upon society's point of view, but upon God's point of view. And it's time to pay particular attention to the God-given personality traits that are as old as *man*kind and *woman*kind. To understand these traits, it's always wise to begin at the beginning.

As a beginning point, we need look no further than the second chapter of Genesis where God stated a simple, straightforward fact. He said, "It is not good for man to be alone" (Genesis 2:18). In this verse, God didn't mince words. He didn't say, "*Sometimes*, it's not good for man to be alone," and He didn't say, "*Maybe* it's not good for man to be alone." He said, "It's not good for a man to be alone." *Period.* This statement is clear-cut; it doesn't leave room for interpretation. The Creator declared that intimate female companionship was (and is) needed by man *for his own good.*

Next, God followed up with a second declaration of equal importance: He said, "I will make for him a helpmate." Think for a moment about the word *helpmate.* What was the Creator saying when He chose that word? Again, the answer is straightforward: God was saying, in no uncertain terms, that *man needs help.*

It's worth noting that we men don't think like that.

We see ourselves as the help*ers*, not the help*ees*. We don't want any advice, any warnings, or any second opinions. We view ourselves as independent operators, problem solvers, autonomous leaders whose authority must never be questioned. When we look in the mirror, we see decision makers, coolheaded commanders in chief capable of surveying the landscape and then boldly going where no man has gone before. We don't need the instruction manual; we don't like committee meetings; we hate asking for directions (even when we're lost). And we don't see the need for *help*, even from a helpmate appointed by God.

We're bulletproof.

Or so we think.

In truth, we do need help, and lots of it. But we don't realize how much help we need or how desperately we need it. In our haste to gain "autonomy" and to preserve our "freedom," we men seem destined to make countless blunders, some great and some small, because we're too hardheaded to accept assistance. So we disregard the implied warning of Genesis 2; we ignore the fact that we need help. And we forget that God has appointed our wives to help us.

A WIFE STRIVES MIGHTILY TO HELP HER HUSBAND BECAUSE THAT'S HOW GOD MADE HER. A WOMAN'S DESIRE TO SUPPORT HER HUSBAND IS SIMPLY A MANIFESTATION OF HER GOD-GIVEN NATURE AS A HELPMATE.

A wife strives mightily to help her husband because that's how God made her. A woman's desire to support her husband is simply a manifestation of her God-given nature as a helpmate. Our wives were created with a natural need to secure, protect, correct, and give advice—*whether we men want it or not*. In fact, the number one complaint that men have about women is that women

IN FACT, THE NUMBER ONE COMPLAINT THAT MEN HAVE ABOUT WOMEN IS THAT WOMEN ARE ALWAYS TRYING TO CONTROL THEM.

are always trying to control them. Women can be subtle, of course, but their messages still manage to get through.

When a woman asks, "Are you going to wear that tie?" she means, "I hope you don't wear that tie."

When a woman asks, "Are you hungry?" she means, "I'm hungry. Let's get something to eat."

"Are you sure you want that parking space?" means, "There's probably a better parking space down front."

A woman's question (which seems harmless to her) may be interpreted by her man as meddling. He likes the tie he picked out (or he wouldn't have picked it out); he's not hungry (or he would have already stopped for food); and he doesn't need help finding a parking place (because he's already spotted a perfectly good one, thank you very much).

What to a woman seems helpful advice can be interpreted by the man as a threat to his authority. What to a woman seems "assisting" is often viewed by the man as "controlling." A woman's subtle hint can be easily mis-interpreted by her man as nagging. But that's usually not how she meant it at all.

Until men understand that their wives have an inter-nal need to help—and until wives begin to understand that their husbands have a built-in "control-detector"—communication inside the marriage will suffer. And as the lines of communication begin to fray, bad things begin to happen. These unfortunate circumstances are entirely preventable if husbands and wives understand two important facts: first, that God created women with an inborn need to help, and second, that men need the help women were cre-ated to give.

Left to their own devices, men some-times behave imma-turely, thus beginning an unfortunate cycle of

> HUSBANDS AND WIVES NEED TO UNDERSTAND TWO IMPORTANT FACTS: FIRST, THAT GOD CREATED WOMEN WITH AN INBORN NEED TO HELP, AND SECOND, THAT MEN NEED THE HELP WOMEN WERE CREATED TO GIVE.

events as the male's desire for independence comes into conflict with the female's God-given urge to help. This cycle is as predictable as it is destructive. Often it begins when the husband does something that his conscience tells him is "borderline" at best. But he does it anyway. Then the wife, who knows her husband better than he knows himself, senses quite correctly that her man needs some sort of

---

MEN AND WOMEN ARE DIFFERENT BECAUSE GOD MADE THEM THAT WAY.

---

midcourse correction. So she communicates this fact, usually (but not always) with words.

The husband—feeling somewhat chastised—becomes resentful. As a way of expressing his "independence" or his "manhood," he digs in his heels and expresses his displeasure (often, but not always) with words. After all, he tells himself, he's the boss.

As the husband's stubbornness increases, so does the wife's innate need to help, usually in the form of more vociferous advice, which the husband misinterprets as harassment. And so the cycle continues, with the husband feeling mistreated and the wife trying to help in the best way she

> HUSBANDS AND WIVES CAN PUT AN END TO THE BICKERING WHEN THEY GENUINELY UNDERSTAND—AND HUMBLY ACKNOWLEDGE—A SIMPLE FACT: MEN AND WOMEN ARE DIFFERENT BECAUSE GOD MADE THEM THAT WAY.

knows how. Things *might* go downhill from there . . . but not necessarily. Husbands and wives can put an end to the bickering when they genuinely understand—and humbly acknowledge—a simple fact: men and women are different because God made them that way.

UNDERSTANDING THE DIFFERENCES

Time and again, the Bible conveys the clear distinction between men and women: their responsibilities, their roles, and even their clothing (Deuteronomy 22:5). God created Adam first, in His own image. Adam represents God's pattern for manhood. Being made in the image of God, Adam had the capacity to know truth, the capacity to recognize moral excellence, and the capacity to exercise his own free will. Adam had the power to choose. Whatever God took out of Adam to create Eve, He never replaced. And whatever God left in Adam, He never put in Eve. So it's not in God's plan for a man to be a woman or vice versa. God intended for the woman to be the completion of *the man in God*—not the competition of *the man only*, nor the competition of *God in the man's life*.

As I've said, it's worth noting again that God gave Adam a job *before* He gave him a wife: "The LORD God took the man and put him in the Garden of Eden to work it and take care of it" (Genesis 2:15 NIV). Adam developed his talent first; he was a career man before he was a family man. That was the pattern that God established.

From the beginning, man defined himself through his vocation and through his ability to achieve results. And very little has changed since then. Men are often more interested in objects and things than in people and feelings. Men still value power, competency, and efficiency; they still experience fulfillment through success and accomplishment *on the job.*

But despite these admirable traits, God looked at Adam and decided that a man, even a man who took his vocation seriously, wasn't enough. Adam was capable, and he was autonomous, but he wasn't accountable. Adam had acquired his talents in solitude. Now it was time to acquire something even more important: character.

> YOU CAN DEVELOP A TALENT WHEN YOU'RE ALONE, BUT YOU CAN DEVELOP CHARACTER ONLY WHEN YOU'RE WITH SOMEONE.

You can develop a talent when you're alone, but you can develop character only when you're with someone. Who you *really* are in life is not found in your skill, your talent, your ability, or your career; it's found in your character.

Character naturally develops sooner in women, who mature more quickly than men do. But that's only one of the differences. Women also tend to be more relationship oriented; their sense of self is defined through their feelings and through the quality of their relationships. More than their male counterparts, women value love, communication, beauty, and community. They experience fulfillment through sharing. They're more interested in harmony, companionship, and loving cooperation. These traits do not occur by accident; they reflect patterns that are as old as the Garden of Eden.

EVE'S FIRST RELATIONSHIP WAS WITH ANOTHER HUMAN BEING. UNLIKE ADAM, SHE NEVER EXPERIENCED SOLITUDE, NOR DID SHE EVER FOCUS SOLELY ON HER WORK.

Eve's first relationship was with another human being. Unlike Adam, she never experienced solitude, nor did she ever focus solely on her work. God established that pattern long ago. Here are a few more traits that are as old as humankind:

- Women believe in collective effort; men often strive for individual success.

- Women tend to focus on relationships; men tend to focus on the task at hand, presuming that everything will be okay "once the problem is fixed."

- Women want to solve problems *together*; men want to solve problems *individually*, by thinking things over in solitude.

- Women tend to approach decisions intuitively; men try to make decisions analytically.

- Women feel the need to improve things (gradually, if necessary); men feel compelled to solve things (once and for all).

- Women seek unanimity within the family or the group; men prefer to act unilaterally, without supervision.

- Women want *to talk* about things first; men want *to fix* things first and talk about it later (if ever).

- Women experience everyday tasks more deeply and are more likely to attribute meaning to everyday events; men are more concerned with checking things off their to-do lists, giving little thought to the deeper meanings of everyday experiences.

Can you begin to see the patterns? Can you see how problems arise when husbands don't understand wives and vice versa? And can you see how changing definitions of marriage have caused chaos for couples who simply cannot reconcile new cultural norms with God's unchanging patterns and principles?

The best thing a woman can do for her husband is to make it easy for him to do the will of God.

—ELISABETH ELLIOT

INTERPRETING THE PATTERN AND DETERMINING YOUR RESPONSE

Recognizing our differences isn't enough. We must also discover how to respond to those differences. As way of getting started, here are five simple strategies for husbands and wives:

1. Giving and Receiving Advice

For Husbands

When it comes to receiving advice, be more accepting of your wife's counsel, recognizing that God created her to be your helpmate.

What's Needed: Humility and Maturity

For Wives

When it comes to giving advice, be sure that your natural tendency to help is reserved for *important* matters, not for *all* matters.

What's Needed: Discernment and Moderation

2. Expressing Emotions

For Husbands

If you'd rather solve problems than express your feelings about those problems, you're not alone. Most men are like that. But as a husband, your duty is clear: to protect your wife physically, financially, and emotionally. So you'll need to learn to express your emotions early and often, even if you'd rather be the strong-and-silent type.

What's Needed: The Willingness to Discuss Feelings

For Wives

If your husband seems emotionally distant, or if he seems focused on work first and everything else second, don't take it personally. God made your man that way. Please remember that your husband may not be ignoring you; he may be trying hard to fix something *by himself.*

    What's Needed: Understanding

3. Everyday Activities

For Husbands

As a man, you've got a to-do list that you think needs to be done *now*. Not so fast! If your wife takes a little longer than you'd prefer, don't be impatient. After all, think of how patient she's been with you.

    What's Needed: Patience

For Wives

When it comes to everyday chores such as shopping, you may like taking your time, and you may misinterpret your husband's impatience as rudeness. In truth, he's only trying to do things the best way he knows how. So be patient with his impatience and respectful of his time.

What's Needed: Empathy

4. Decision Making

For Husbands

When you're about to make a major decision, remember that God designed your wife to help you. You'll make better decisions if you ask for her opinion first.

What's Needed: Humility and a Spirit of Cooperation

For Wives

When your husband doesn't ask for your opinion first, remember that God designed your man to be decisive, and sometimes he's going to be *very* decisive.

    What's Needed: Understanding

5. The Need for Both Solitude and Togetherness

For Husbands

Before you retreat to your man cave and zone out, check in with your wife. She may need your companionship, and as her protector, you shouldn't ignore—or resent—her needs.

    What's Needed: Concern and Unselfishness

For Wives

When you feel the need for your husband's companionship, don't expect him to be a mind reader—tell him how you feel, and find positive ways to communicate your needs. The tone and timing of your communication will determine how he responds. Together you both can find a balance between solitude and together time.

What's Needed: Cooperation and Positive Communication

———◇———

After God created Eve, He made yet another declaration: In a single, elegant sentence, the Creator summed up the institution of marriage. God said, "Therefore shall a man leave his father and his mother, and shall cleave unto his wife: and they shall be one flesh" (Gen 2:24 KJV).

With this pronouncement, God endorsed the traditional marriage: a man and a woman, holding tightly to each other, becoming as one.

In today's temptation-filled world, "becoming as one" is relatively easy, but holding tightly to each other for a lifetime is considerably harder. Holding to the principles we find in Scripture and being mindful of patterns in human behavior will help us build and maintain that lifetime bond.

So what sort of man does it take to be the kind of husband that God expects and women want?

It starts with maturity.

— QUESTIONS FOR REFLECTION —

Did the strategies in this chapter strike you as helpful? In what ways do you see them playing out in your own relationship?

_____

_____

_____

_____

_____

_____

_____

_____

_____

_____

_____

_____

_____

_____

_____

_____

_____

_____

_____

_____

_____

_____

_____

_____

_____

_____

_____

_____

_____

_____

— PRAYER —

FOR MEN: Dear God, I know You uniquely made my wife and me in Your image. Help me to celebrate the differences between us and allow us to come together with our own strengths and weaknesses to be stronger together. In Your name I pray, Amen.

FOR WOMEN: Dear God, please help me to love and accept the differences between my husband and me. Help us to celebrate them and, as a team, become stronger together than by ourselves. In Your name I pray, Amen.

— 4 —

TRAIT #1: MATURITY

"Maturity is when you stop making excuses and start making changes."
—Anonymous

Every woman craves relationship with a real man. Think about it. She might be temporarily satisfied with someone less mature, but at the end of the day, a woman wants to be with a Real Man.

That's why I believe the first essential trait all women want from a man is maturity. The patterns and principles given by the Creator to mankind at the dawn of human history form the foundation of a successful life *and* a successful marriage. The Word of God is our source of faith, and our rule of conduct is based upon these principles. For those who choose to study the Bible in depth, the message becomes clear: God's universe unfolds in a specific way, according to His perfect design. When we accept the Creator's blueprint and live by it, we are blessed. When we do otherwise, we bear the cost.

We should study Scripture in order to understand the principles that God is trying to teach us and discover the patterns He wants us to know. Once we comprehend these universal laws, we can take the things we've learned and weave them into the fabric of our daily lives.

Now remember, God does everything according to a pattern and based on a principle.

A principle is a broad and basic truth, a permanent feature on the human landscape; it doesn't change with popular culture or social mores. Even if societal values shift, even if cultural norms are completely overturned, even if an entire population believes otherwise, God's principles cannot be altered. His laws are as old as time itself. His truths never change.

One of our Father's basic principles has to

> GOD'S PRINCIPLES CANNOT BE ALTERED. HIS LAWS ARE AS OLD AS TIME ITSELF. HIS TRUTHS NEVER CHANGE.

do with maturity—what
maturity is and what it
isn't. So let me make one
thing clear at the outset:

> GOD DOES EVERYTHING
> ACCORDING TO A PATTERN
> AND BASED ON A PRINCIPLE.

growing older isn't the same thing as growing up. As Edwin
Louis Cole noted, "Being a male is a matter of birth. Being
a man is a matter of choice." Many grown-ups behave like
children, and vice versa. In truth, the process of growing up
has remarkably little to do with the aging process.

Maturity doesn't come with age; it begins with the acceptance of responsibility.

Gloria is a successful intellectual property attorney.
At a lunch meeting with her and another highly successful developer in New York, we talked about Gloria's
experience with her ex-husband. These are her words:

I just wish he would grow up!

*"When we met he was so eager to marry and
start a family. However, upon reflection, it seems he*

MATURITY DOESN'T COME WITH AGE; IT BEGINS WITH THE ACCEPTANCE OF RESPONSIBILITY.

was more interested in the appearance of a responsible family man rather than truly being one. He wanted the fanfare of a fabulous island wedding, to impress others with letters to his unborn son, to decorate the nursery, curate a sneaker collection for his future fashion icon. He often spoke of how he would be present unlike his own father. However, within months after our son's birth, his promises and visions of fatherhood seemed to erode.

"He was unable or unwilling to self-regulate for the good of our family and impulse seemed to dictate every decision around money or time. Financially, he was irresponsible. I leveraged my credit to secure a business loan for him and support his dreams. He used that loan partially for the business and partially to court other women with expensive dinners and shoes and to buy expensive watches and other luxury goods

for himself. He was more concerned with building his appearance of wealth than building real wealth for our family. Each poor decision he made compromised our ability to create the life we had imagined together before marriage. It will take five years postdivorce for us to settle that debt, and now we're that much further behind in saving for our son's college tuition.

"As for allocating time with our son, I don't believe he has made the sacrifices that come with the decision to parent a child. While he is certainly more present than his father was in his life, and I am so grateful that he has a loving relationship with our son, he parents out of convenience. Although he has two weekends a month with our son, he feels unable to commit to a set schedule because of his work schedule. Rather than committing to a schedule and missing the social or 'work' events that might happen on those four days of the month, he fits our son in when it's convenient for him. He would argue that he must

be present with his business clients or he could risk losing their business, which would then compromise his ability to provide financially for our son.

"Conversely, I am always parenting whether convenient or not. When his schedule changes or our son is sick, I'm the one having to figure it out and make alternate plans. I too am a working professional with many demands on my time. I am often perplexed that my ex-husband never asks if he can make alternate arrangements for our son even if it means changing his plans. He just assumes, rightfully or wrongfully, that I will handle it.

"I just wish he would grow up and fully be a present father whether convenient or not."

Maturity isn't a function of the calendar; it's a matter of accountability. We don't begin to mature until we accept personal responsibility for our words, our thoughts, our motives, our actions, and our attitudes.

So a sixty-year-old who refuses to accept responsibility is less mature than a twenty-year-old who does.

People who hold themselves accountable tend to grow up in a hurry. They expect more of themselves, they make fewer mistakes, they get things done, and they lead by example. These folks are the "grown-ups in the room," not the perpetual Peter Pans who continuously deflect accountability.

Here's a simple formula for growing up, whatever your age: accept personal responsibility for the things you say, the thoughts you think, and the things you do. If you make a mistake (which you inevitably will from time to time), don't blame your society, or your culture, or your friends, or your family; look only to the person whose face appears in the mirror.

"Real maturity means having zero tolerance for anything that is not of God."

—VIVIAN C.

When you steadfastly refuse to blame others—when you step up and assume responsibility for the things you do and the results you achieve—you'll transform yourself from child to adult. This transformation may take time, and it may seem difficult at first, but it's well worth the effort because perpetual childhood is difficult, costly, and an unsatisfying way to live.

MATURITY REQUIRES CHANGE

Edwin Louis Cole observed that, "Change is the only constant in maturity." And he was right. In order to mature, men and women must be willing to change—there's simply no other way to grow up. To mature spiritually and emotionally, people must change the way they speak, the way they think, and the way they behave. But some folks simply aren't willing to do that. They'd prefer to stay stuck in adolescence, operating under the mistaken belief that the teenage years are the best years. These perpetual "youngsters" seem determined to behave like juveniles, even if the birth certificate says they're old enough to collect Social Security.

You can always tell when people haven't matured because they're using the same words they've always used, expressing the same opinions they've always expressed, thinking the same thoughts, and being guided by the same motives. They're engaging in the same actions, and they're displaying the same attitudes. If you knew them in high school, you know them today because the only thing that's changed since then is the number of years they've been on the planet. Otherwise, it's the same ol' same old.

When people become stuck in a teenage state of mind, they tend to behave impulsively; they tend to shirk responsibility; they tend to cut corners and push limits, hoping not to get caught. But eventually they *do* get caught. Yet even then, when the consequences of bad behavior become apparent, their response is predictably

immature. Instead of accepting responsibility (and learning a lesson), immature people complain loudly about the
unfairness of it all and blame somebody else. These perpetual teenagers may grow old, but they never grow up.

"My husband is mature, which means he isn't interested in 'bad boy' behavior. He has a strong sense
of who he is, so he isn't influenced by other people's
negative behavior."

—KERRY B.

Behaving immaturely seems fun, *at first*. Avoiding
responsibility seems easy, *for a while*. And the good
times do indeed roll, *temporarily*. But the good times
don't last forever because life isn't a perpetual party,
no matter what the perpetual partiers may think. As it
turns out, immaturity is expensive. Very expensive.

The costs of immaturity accrue day by day, month
by month, and year by year. And when the bill finally

comes due, it must be
paid not only by the
person who racked up
the debt, but also by

SO IT'S NO WONDER, THEN, THAT
MATURITY IS FIRST THING THAT
WOMEN WANT IN A MAN.

the family members who must try, as best they can, to
repair the damage.

So it's no wonder, then, that maturity is first thing
that women want in a man. Wise women want to spend
their lives with fully grown men, not with aging adoles-
cents. Women want men who are willing to change.

Change is the essence of maturation. You'll never
mature in life unless you're willing to change. You may
live to be one hundred years old, but if you're still behaving like a ten-year-old, you're not fully grown.

Rick Warren observed, "Change always starts in your
mind. The way you think determines the way you feel,
and the way you feel influences the way you act." Simply
put, thoughts precede actions. When you begin thinking
like an adult, you'll begin behaving like one, too.

"If we don't change, we don't grow. If we don't grow, we aren't really living."

—GAIL M.

The possibility for change begins the moment you realize you still have much to learn. But not everybody thinks that way. People who think they already know it all see no reason to learn, no reason to grow, no reason to mature. People who think they have all the answers probably aren't even asking the *right questions*. If a person says, "It's my way or the highway," the way in question probably has plenty of potholes. One of those potholes is a personality trait that's a permanent impediment to spiritual growth and emotional health. That trait is stubbornness.

Stubborn people will always be ignorant people. Why? Because they refuse to even contemplate the possibility of change. It doesn't matter how much money they have or how much power they wield. Stubborn people refuse to adapt, and they refuse to learn because they mistakenly believe that they already know everything that needs to be known. So they remain trapped in a cycle of immaturity and destructiveness.

Stubborn people are compelled to deny personal responsibility. To do otherwise would be to admit that their way *isn't* the right way. So, they maintain (wrongly) that it's always the other guy's fault. Instead of acknowledging truth and searching for solutions, stubborn folks refute reality by shifting the blame elsewhere. This pass-the-buck strategy actually works for a while, but eventually the truth does what it always does: the truth reveals itself for all the world to see. That's when the price of stubbornness must be paid in full.

To avoid the consequences of stubbornness, you must be willing to change. But

> YOU WILL NEVER CHANGE UNTIL YOU'RE WILLING TO CONFRONT THE TRUTH ABOUT YOUR WORDS, YOUR THOUGHTS, YOUR MOTIVES, YOUR ACTIONS, AND YOUR ATTITUDES.

you will never change until you're willing to confront the truth about your words, your thoughts, your motives, your actions, and your attitudes. Unless you are willing to assess yourself objectively (and often), you'll keep making the same old mistakes and suffering the same old consequences that result from the same poor decisions.

To make mature decisions you need two things: values and principles.

VALUES AND PRINCIPLES

Your values are those things that you consider most important in life. Values are the things you stand for. Values are the things you'll pay the price for, perhaps the ultimate price. In the most extreme situations, you'll be willing

> VALUES ARE THE THINGS YOU STAND FOR. VALUES ARE THE THINGS YOU'LL PAY THE PRICE FOR, PERHAPS THE ULTIMATE PRICE.

to die for the values you hold dear. Dr. King said that if a man doesn't have something to die for, he has nothing to live for. How true. If you're guided by the values that God promises to reward, you'll reap the blessings that He has promised to those who choose to obey Him. But if the things you value are not from God, no amount of wishful thinking will spare you from the consequences.

Principles are the set of moral rules that help you determine right from wrong. Principles help you define the things that add to your life (the assets) and avoid the things that take away from your life (the liabilities). Some principles are straightforward; others are not. The devil lives in the gray area.

> PRINCIPLES ARE THE SET OF MORAL RULES THAT HELP YOU DETERMINE RIGHT FROM WRONG. PRINCIPLES HELP YOU DEFINE THE THINGS THAT ADD TO YOUR LIFE (THE ASSETS) AND AVOID THE THINGS THAT TAKE AWAY FROM YOUR LIFE (THE LIABILITIES).

It's easy to make decisions when things are black or

white. It's simple to make the right call when the facts are clear, when the consequences are certain, and when the results are predetermined. But when the lines between right and wrong become blurred, the devil gains a foothold and temptation appears, sometimes out of nowhere. Satan (often disguised as *someone* or *something* that looks *very* attractive) knocks on your door and makes you an offer. To avoid trouble, you must say *no* to Satan's sales pitch by resisting the temptation he's placed on your doorstep. To resist that temptation quickly and confidently, you'll need a set of principles that you've acquired *in advance*.

"Apply God's principles, keep your heart pure, and you will succeed."

—EDWIN LOUIS COLE

The principles you need to navigate through life aren't deep, dark secrets known only to a few. Nor are these concepts difficult to understand. To the contrary, the principles that God wants you to live by are the same rules for life that you were taught as a child. Over the years, you've heard these truths time and again from parents and grandparents, from teachers and preachers, from friends, family members, and mentors. Not surprisingly, these are the same concepts that you encounter whenever you study your Bible. These principles are so familiar that we've developed popular sayings that sum them up, such as "You reap what you sow," "Two wrongs don't make a right," "Actions speak louder than words," "There's no time like the present," and "Honesty is the best policy." These are but a few of the truisms that, while they may seem trite (because you've heard them so often), serve as essential guidelines for life.

You can think of these principles as tools that make up a mental toolkit, a toolkit that you acquire throughout life and carry with you wherever you go. The better your tools, the better your results. And the best time to acquire these tools is *before* you need them, not *when* you need them.

Why?

I'm glad you asked.

You need to fill up your cognitive toolkit *sooner* rather than *later* because when the time comes to make an important decision or to resist an almost-irresistible temptation, it's too late to start looking around for the principles that apply. When the moment comes to make a quality decision, you may not have time to pull out a textbook, or to reach for your Bible, or to call your mentor on the phone. When Satan shows up at your doorstep, it's just the two of you, face-to-face. And because your adversary is a savvy salesman, he'll try to make the sale now, not later.

> MATURE PEOPLE THINK
> LONG-TERM.

The difference between a good decision and a bad one often can be traced back to the core principles

that guide the person
who's deciding. Ma-
ture people know what
they stand for, and they

> MATURE PEOPLE KNOW WHAT
> THEY STAND FOR, AND THEY
> KNOW IT IN ADVANCE.

know it in advance. They think long term. They consider not only the potential benefits of a decision, but
also the potential costs.

**As passions subside after the initial infatuation, dedi-
cation to each other's welfare and happiness emerge as
the major binding forces in a relationship.**

—AARON BECK

Mature men and women look before they leap,
not after. They recognize a dangerous temptation, even
when it's wrapped in a very appealing package. They
make high-quality decisions based on non-changing
principles that they learned along the way *and* managed
to put into practice.

James 1:22 (NLT) offers this timeless (and timely) advice: "But don't just listen to God's word. You must do what it says. Otherwise, you are only fooling yourselves." James understood that it's not enough *to know* what's right or *to talk* about what's right; you've also got *to do* what's right.

> IT'S NOT ENOUGH *TO KNOW* WHAT'S RIGHT OR *TO TALK* ABOUT WHAT'S RIGHT; YOU'VE ALSO GOT *TO DO* WHAT'S RIGHT.

So don't be satisfied to learn or to recite the wisdom of the ages. Make whatever changes are necessary *to live* by those rules, seven days a week, twenty-four hours a day. Make "practice what you preach" one of the principles that you live by. While you're at it, take an honest look at the things you've been doing and way you've been living. If change is required, start making those changes today.

If you think that you're a little too "set in your ways" to change your ways, you're wrong. The old saying "You can't teach an old dog new tricks" may apply to canines, but it certainly doesn't apply to you. You're never too old to grow spiritually or emotionally, and if you can still feel your pulse, you can be sure that God has an important plan for your life.

Albert Einstein famously said, "Insanity is doing the same thing over and over again and expecting different results." If you'd like better results, you'll need to do some things differently than you did in the past. To do things differently, you'll need to think differently and act differently. In other words, you'll need to keep growing and maturing every day of your life.

As you continue to mature, you'll eventually begin reaping the long-term rewards of improved decision making—which brings me to the next thing that God expects from a man. It's the same thing women want from a man.

They want decisiveness.

— QUESTIONS FOR REFLECTION —

MAN: What values and principles matter most to you? Think about a recent time in your life when you made a significant change. Which core values and principles helped you navigate that change with maturity?

WOMEN: Think about ways in which your man consistently demonstrates maturity. What principles and values does he exemplify to you?

_____

_____

_____

_____

_____

_____

_____

_____

TRAIT #1: MATURITY

_____

_____

_____

_____

_____

_____

_____

_____

_____

_____

_____

_____

_____

_____

_____

_____

_____

_____

— PRAYERS —

MAN: Dear God, help me navigate the changes in life with maturity so that my wife can look to me for comfort in such times. Help me to pause and make use of my spiritual toolkit to help do the right thing in all situations and handle adversity with maturity. I pray this in Your name, Amen.

WOMAN: Dear God, help me encourage and support my husband and walk in Your ways. When change comes, help me to look to him as my safe haven. In Your name I pray, Amen.

— 5 —

TRAIT #2: DECISIVENESS

Living is a constant process of deciding
what we are going to do next.

—José Ortega y Gasset

Have you ever encountered a man who lacks decisiveness? If so, you know he's not someone a good woman wants to be yoked to for life. A woman wants to be with a partner who will not struggle with decision making. She wants a man who makes *quality* decisions quickly and confidently. Such a man has the knack for taking the right path, the wisdom to make the correct choice, and the foresight to select the best opportunities.

Decisiveness is insight in action. It's the ability *to know* what's right and, just as important, it's the willingness *to do* what's right.

Decisive people make good leaders because they arrive at the correct solution sooner rather than later. They have a profound distaste for delay; when a decision needs to be made, they make it. But they don't stop there. Decisive leaders also possess the courage to *act* upon their decisions and thus avoid the trap of procrastination.

Decisiveness is an acquired skill that many people never bother to acquire. Since the days of Adam and Eve, poor decision making has been part of the human condition. But in today's temptation-filled world, it's easier than ever to make poor choices. As a result, bad behavior has reached epidemic proportions. Everywhere we look, or so it seems, people are doing crazy things and reaping the bitter consequences. We need look no further than our own neighborhoods to see the results of the poor choices that plague our homes and our society.

We see drug addictions, alcohol addictions, food

> DECISIVENESS IS INSIGHT IN ACTION. IT'S THE ABILITY TO KNOW WHAT'S RIGHT AND, JUST AS IMPORTANTLY, IT'S THE WILLINGNESS TO DO WHAT'S RIGHT.

addictions, and gambling addictions, for starters. We see too many young people who desperately need the benefits of education instead treating school as if it were a decade-long paid vacation, just killing time until that fateful day they can finally drop out. We see the gradual disintegration of traditional family values depriving too many children of the guidance they need to make good choices. So it's no wonder that our jails are overflowing, our penitentiaries are packed, and our super-max prisons are maxed out. The inmates who reside there not only are serving time; they're also living out the consequences of the very poor choices they made *before* they were incarcerated.

So what's the answer? As a society—and as individuals—we must replace poor choices with good ones. We must replace unhealthy habits with helpful ones. And we must replace impulsivity with wisdom. To do so, we need decisive men and women who can see the world clearly, make accurate assessments, and take appropriate action at the appropriate time. Thankfully, we need look no further than God's Word for guidance.

> "Whoever is on God's side is on the winning side, and whoever is on the other side cannot win. There is no chance, no gamble. There is freedom to choose which side we shall be on, but no freedom to negotiate the results."
>
> —A. W. TOZER

Perhaps you've made poor decisions in the past; maybe you've done things you're not proud of or been in relationships that caused you great pain. Maybe Old Man Trouble has visited your house so often that you feel like he's a member of the family. After one too many setbacks, perhaps you just don't trust your own judgment anymore. If so, you've come to resemble the baseball manager Casey Stengel, who famously said, "I made up my mind, but I made it up both ways." And that's a problem.

Indecision results in paralysis, which inevitably morphs into unhappiness. People who

> PEOPLE WHO AVOID MAKING DECISIONS FIND THEMSELVES CONSTANTLY TIED UP IN EMOTIONAL KNOTS.

avoid making decisions find themselves constantly tied up in emotional knots. Oftentimes, they're so focused on pleasing everybody (an impossible task) that they fail to focus on pleasing God. Or instead of doing the right thing—and letting the chips fall where they may—they do nothing. William James was correct when he observed, "There is no more miserable human being than the one in whom nothing is habitual but indecision."

Perhaps you think that decisiveness is a gift given to only a few, and that God withheld that gift from you. But if you think that, you're mistaken. Decisiveness is a skill that can be enhanced, improved, and refined *if* you begin at the beginning: God's Word.

DECISIVENESS IS A SKILL THAT CAN BE ENHANCED, IMPROVED, AND REFINED IF YOU BEGIN AT THE BEGINNING: GOD'S WORD.

In the first chapter of James, God offers a clear warning to indecisive, lukewarm, double-minded believers:

If you need wisdom, ask our generous God, and he will give it to you. He will not rebuke you for asking. But when you ask him, be sure that your faith is in God alone. Do not waver, for a person with divided loyalty is as unsettled as a wave of the sea that is blown and tossed by the wind. Such people should not expect to receive anything from the Lord. Their loyalty is divided between God and the world, and they are unstable in everything they do (1:5–8 NLT).

The message is clear: you can't expect God to help you make quality decisions quickly and confidently if you're using the world's value system as your guide. And as long as you trust the world's guidance system first and God's guidance next, you'll always be conflicted; you'll often make poor choices, and you'll never be content. In order to make better choices—and to make them in a timely manner—you must develop a set of values and principles that guide your decision-making process.

Values, as I've stated previously, are the things that are most important to you: the things you're willing to live for and die for. You may think that your values are straightforward. You may believe that the things you stand for are the tried-and-true clichéd values that everybody talks about: things like family, health, integrity, and faith. But here's a word of warning: your *real* values are reflected in the things you *do*, not the things you *say*.

It's easy to talk about high-sounding values; almost everybody does it. We human beings love talking about the noble things we value because talking about them makes us look good. But it's considerably easier to verbalize those values than it is to live by them. Talk, as the old saying goes, is cheap, and that goes for self-talk, too. Often, we talk ourselves into believing that certain things are important to us, yet our behaviors reveal different priorities.

So if you really want to look at your own motivations, you'll need to examine your actions, not your proclamations.

I have a simple two-step diagnostic tool that unfailingly reveals people's *true* values (not the values they crow about). Step One concerns money; Step Two concerns time. So here's my easy-to-use, two-step value-detector:

Step One: Look at the person's bank account.

Step Two: Look at the person's calendar.

If you tell me how you spend your money and your time, I'll tell you what your *real* values are.

IF YOU TELL ME HOW YOU SPEND YOUR MONEY AND YOUR TIME, I'LL TELL YOU WHAT YOUR REAL VALUES ARE.

Over the years, I've counseled countless couples who were

trying to patch things up. During all those years, through all those mentoring sessions, I've never encountered a husband or wife who said, "Pastor, I'm not *really* committed to my marriage. I've got more important things to do."

To the contrary, people always proclaim their near-total commitment to their families and to their marriage. They say things like "My marriage is the most important thing in the world to me," or "I'd do anything to keep my family together," or "I can't stand the thought of hurting our kids."

These proclamations sound noble, but when I ask couples how they spend their money and their time, I discover that *many* things seem to have a higher priority than the marriage. For starters, money is more important (because that's something they argue about most). TV is more important (because that's where they spend most of their free time—and to make matters worse, they don't even watch the same shows!). Social media is more important (because that's how they keep up with their friends). Spectator sports are more important (because at least one spouse happens to be a "rabid" fan). Even immature pastimes like partying-with-the-guys or girl's-nights-out are more important (because for some reason, husbands and wives feel it's their inalienable right to "blow off steam" *without* their spouses).

It's no wonder, then, that marriage begins to take a backseat. After taking time for TV, social media, spectator sports, and hanging out with the guys (or girls), there's simply not enough time or money left to go around. When couples spend copious amounts of time away from each other, and when they spend most of their disposable income on things that separate them from each other, marital troubles inevitably accumulate.

"If you say that a relationship is important—and if you mean what you say—you'll *gladly* invest the money and the time that's required to make it work.

To do so, you'll need to take control of your own calendar."

IF YOU SAY THAT A RELATIONSHIP IS IMPORTANT—AND IF YOU MEAN WHAT YOU SAY—YOU'LL *GLADLY* INVEST THE MONEY AND THE TIME THAT'S REQUIRED TO MAKE IT WORK.

Everything important to me goes on my calendar, including family time. You may be saying to yourself, "Pastor, that sounds *cold.*" It may sound cold, but it's not. I've learned that if I don't set my own priorities, other people will set them for me. And since my family is a vitally important priority to me, I schedule family time, right there in black and white, on my daily to-do list.

Every day my calendar speaks to me. It says, "Pastor Bernard, remember this. These things are important." That's why I also schedule workout times. My health is important to me. If your health is

IF I DON'T SET MY OWN PRIORITIES, OTHER PEOPLE WILL SET THEM FOR ME.

important to you, you'll carve out time for exercise, too. After all, your body is on loan, and it has an expiration date. Keep it fresh as long as you can.

Is your faith important? Then you need to make a standing appointment with God every morning, even if it means setting the alarm clock a few minutes earlier. God doesn't need the appointment with you (He's already got everything figured out); you need the appointment with Him. He's always available, and His Word is right there on your bookshelf, computer, or smart phone app. The rest is up to you.

As you read these words, you may be thinking, "I'm already slammed, and now Pastor Bernard wants me to add more things to my list. Family. Exercise. Daily devotional time. There's no way!"

If that's what you're thinking, here are some questions worth pondering: How much TV are you watching? How much time are you spending (wasting) on social media? What about the time you spend hanging out with casual acquaintances? And what about the time (and money) you spend following your favorite sports team? None of these activities, when pursued in moderation, is a vice. But they're dangerous to your spiritual health *if* they interfere with higher priorities like faith, family, and physical health.

What you do speaks so loudly that I cannot hear what you say.

—RALPH WALDO EMERSON

If I were to look at your calendar and your bank account today, would I know what you stand for? Would your friends and family know? Or is your life so blurred that people can't tell where you stand, what you stand for, and where you're headed? These questions deserve to be answered, and you deserve the experience of answering them.

THE RULES OF THE GAME

You can think of values as the "what" and principles as the "how."

Values are *what* you stand for. They're the things you live for and the things you're willing to die for.

Principles are the timeless truths, the practical instructions, the rules of the game that all of humanity must play by. Principles show you *how* to apply your values and *how* to accomplish you goals. But beware: not all principles are created equal.

The world offers its own set of principles, which inevitably prove to be untrue. The world promises "something for nothing," "consequence-free sin," and countless other free-lunch temptations that are hazardous to your emotional, financial, physical, and marital health. The world says that you can have it all without paying for it all, and that when the bill comes due, the world says that you can refinance everything and keep right on spending.

God's principles, on the other hand, make no such promises. God doesn't promise free lunches or consequence-free misbehavior. He says that you'll need to work for the things you want, and He warns that if you behave badly, you'll have to pay someday soon. God's principles work because that's how He designed His world to work. In God's universe, actions have reactions, behaviors have results, good seeds yield good harvests, and bad seeds don't.

> GOD DOESN'T PROMISE FREE LUNCHES OR CONSEQUENCE-FREE MISBEHAVIOR. HE SAYS THAT YOU'LL NEED TO WORK FOR THE THINGS YOU WANT, AND HE WARNS THAT IF YOU BEHAVE BADLY, YOU'LL HAVE TO PAY SOMEDAY SOON.

God's principles are your roadmap to success because they help you distinguish between the things that add to your life (the assets) and the things that take away from your life (the liabilities).

These are people who add to my life—they're assets:

_____

_____

_____

_____

_____

_____

_____

These are the people who detract from my life—they're liabilities:

_____

_____

_____

_____

_____

_____

_____

These are the habits that improve my life—they're assets:

_____

_____

_____

_____

_____

_____

These are the habits that detract from my life—they're liabilities:

_____

_____

_____

_____

_____

_____

_____

These are the attitudes that enhance my life—they're assets:

_____

_____

_____

_____

_____

_____

_____

These are the attitudes that constrict my life—they're liabilities:

_____

_____

_____

_____

_____

_____

_____

These are the activities that, by their very nature, make me a better person—they're assets:

_____

_____

_____

_____

_____

_____

These activities have the potential to destroy everything I hold dear—they're liabilities.

_____

_____

_____

_____

_____

_____

Some liabilities are like a mortgage (long-term debt). The bill keeps coming due, month after month, year after year. Other liabilities are like a payday loan; the bill comes due in a day or two, whether you're ready or not. Either way, life's liabilities eventually must be paid because that's how the world works.

Unless you're discerning, you may rush into relationships that create big liabilities. If you do, you'll start making decisions that have long-term consequences. Some decisions are reversible; some aren't. When it comes to the irreversible kind, I suggest that you take plenty of time to make up your mind, since a single decision can shackle you for years to come. Be cautious before committing yourself to any time-consuming association that has the potential to become a rapidly depreciating asset. Look before you leap. The bigger the decision, the longer you should look. In life, your liabilities add up. Society keeps score.

When it comes to judging which people are

liabilities and which ones are assets, there are no guar-
antees. But if you keep your eyes wide open and know
what to look for, you can begin to see patterns. And
you can learn, once and for all, that in assessing human
beings, appearances are, indeed, deceiving. (There it is
again: "All that glitters is not gold.")

Some people are very good at concealing their true
motives. They make you think it's all about *you* when it's
really all about *them*. That's why you need to be wise,
discerning, and observant in your relationships. And
you need to be a good listener because people do eventually tell you about themselves (by the things they say
and the things they do). But folks won't tell you about
themselves if they can't get a word in edgewise.

Speaking of conversations, I'll let you in on a little
secret: *I'm not available on demand.* People can't just call
me on the phone, expect me to answer, and then make
a last-minute appointment. Once again, you may be
thinking, "Pastor, that sounds *cold*." But my insistence

on managing my calendar isn't cold; it's based on a principle: a *Biblical* principle.

In The Living Bible, Psalm 90:12 is translated: "Teach us to number our days and recognize how few they are; help us to spend them as we should." What God is telling us in this verse is yet another principle: "Life here on earth is brief, so there's not time for everything."

When, as the old hymn goes, "The trumpet of the Lord shall sound and time shall be no more," I'll have plenty of time to talk to anybody about anything. Meanwhile, here on planet earth, I know that God wants me to treat time like the nonrenewable resource that it is. That means I can't be all things to all people. And neither can you.

If I allow other people to organize my life, I can't be sure that they'll spend *my time* wisely. So I guard my calendar like a guard my wallet: *very* carefully. I advise you to do the same.

Time is the coin of your life, and only you can determine how it will be spent. Be careful lest you let other people spend it for you.

—CARL SANDBERG

By controlling my calendar, I'm taking charge of a priceless treasure gifted by God: time. Every day I take time to seek His guidance. Then when I'm armed with His wisdom and His Word, I start making decisions, which is precisely what God wants me to do. I know that He will *guide* my decision making, but He won't *dictate* my decisions.

Of course, I believe in the supernatural. As a Christian, I believe in miracles, both large and small. But I also understand how God set things up: He gave us His Word filled with values and principles that guide our actions. But He also gave us free will, and He gave us the opportunity to grow up. Or not.

Growing up means making our own decisions. But

if you're a religious person, you may be tempted to ask God to make every decision for you. You may ask, "God, is this the person I should marry?" Or, "Lord, is this the right job for me?" Or you may ask countless other questions of your Creator, trying to pass the burden of decision making on to Him.

But here in the real world, it doesn't work that way. God gives you the patterns and principles through the teachings found in His Holy Word. Therein you'll find everything you need to make quality decisions quickly and confidently. The rest is up to you.

> GOD GIVES YOU THE PATTERNS AND PRINCIPLES THROUGH THE TEACHINGS FOUND IN HIS HOLY WORD. THEREIN YOU'LL FIND EVERYTHING YOU NEED TO MAKE QUALITY DECISIONS QUICKLY AND CONFIDENTLY. THE REST IS UP TO YOU.

You see, God gave you a mind for a very good reason: *to use it*. If He'd wanted to dictate your every move, He could have done so. But that wasn't the way God treated Adam, and it's not the way He's going to treat you. When it comes to life's toughest questions, God wants you to decide. Adam was given the ability to make choices. You're made in the same way. God gave you free will because He wanted to create a human being, not a robot.

So don't be superstitious. Be practical. I cannot tell you how liberating it is no longer to live in fear of making wrong decisions or not being in the will of God! Decision making is a skill you develop over time. It requires wisdom, discernment, good judgment, and learning from your mistakes!

———◇———

Edwin Louis Cole observed, "A man who honors God privately will show it by making good decisions publicly." That's the kind of man God is looking for; it also happens to be the kind of man women want and need.

But it's getting harder and harder for men *or* women to make good decisions publicly *or* privately. There are so many distractions and so many temptations. The devil has always been a hard worker, but today he's got more tools than ever before.

The warning of 1 Peter 5:8 is clear: "Be sober, be vigilant; because your adversary the devil walks about like a roaring lion, seeking whom he may devour" (NKJV). Satan comes—often quietly at first—to steal, to kill, and to destroy. He wants you to have distorted values, he wants you to employ the wrong principles, and he wants you to make disastrous decisions. If the devil can wreck your life and destroy your spirit, he will. My former pastor said, "If you give the devil a stick, he ought to beat you with it." Don't help the devil destroy your life. Poverty, confusion, sickness, and temptations are waiting for opportunities to claim your marriage, your health, your sanity, and your children. Life is a fight for territory. When you stop fighting for what you want, what you *don't want* will take over the territory.

Every life, including yours, is a struggle for territory. God is leading you to level ground while the devil is beckoning you toward the slippery slope. The temptations are real, and they're dangerous. That's why you need the protection afforded by values and principles pleasing to God. If you ask for His guidance, you will receive it. If you seek, you will find. But please remember this: finding is reserved for the seekers.

How long must we stand at the door and knock before we *finally* acquire the wisdom we so desperately need? God doesn't say (of course, things would be easier if He did). If God said, "Keep knocking for an hour and the door will be opened," most of us would keep knocking. Or if He said, "You've got to knock for seven days," we could probably hold it together for that long. Maybe longer.

But God doesn't get into specifics. He just promises

to answer *sometime*. And we must trust that He'll keep that promise. So if you sincerely want to become a more decisive person who makes high-quality choices sooner rather than later, start knocking today. Keep knocking. And don't give up. If you continue to seek, you can be sure that one day—*perhaps this very day*—the Lord will open that door, reveal His plans, and transform your life.

— QUESTIONS FOR REFLECTION —

What are some things about which you struggle to be decisive? What can you do to find some clarity? How are you spending the majority of your time and money? Are there ways you can improve? Write out how you spend time and money and see if you can make some changes—do you think this will allow you more clarity to make decisions?

_____

_____

_____

_____

_____

_____

_____

_____

_____

_____

_____

_____

_____

_____

_____

_____

_____

_____

_____

_____

_____

_____

_____

_____

— PRAYER —

FOR MEN: Dear God, help me to be decisive—to find the time and energy to make the right decisions and to consult Your Word for truth. In Your name I pray, Amen.

FOR WOMEN: Dear God, Help me to encourage and support my husband in his decisions and look to you as the director of our paths. In Your name I pray, Amen.

— 6 —

TRAIT #3: CONSISTENCY

Character is a simple habit long continued.

—Plutarch

Over the years, I've seen many women struggle when their husbands lack consistency. It's a trait they crave because God built it into their very core. Consistency is firmness of character. It's the ability to make mature, quality decisions time and again, facing down the inevitable temptations that Satan scatters across your path. And when it comes to mature, *consistent* decision making, here's another

DECISIONS ARE NOT MADE IN A MOMENT OF TIME; THEY'RE ROOTED IN YOUR CHARACTER.

principle worth remembering: decisions are not made in a moment of time; they're rooted in your character.

D. L. Moody famously said, "Character is what you are in the dark." Pastor Moody understood that it's relatively easy to maintain one's character when the sun is shining and everybody's watching, but that the real test is how a man behaves when he thinks (wrongly) that nobody is watching.

Consistency requires congruence between values and actions. When your actions are in sync with your values, you can look people in the eye, knowing what you stand for. When your values match your actions, peace occurs naturally— peace in your home *and* peace in your heart. When there's congruence between the things you

> CONSISTENCY REQUIRES CONGRUENCE BETWEEN VALUES AND ACTIONS. WHEN YOUR ACTIONS ARE IN SYNC WITH YOUR VALUES, YOU CAN LOOK PEOPLE IN THE EYE, KNOWING WHAT YOU STAND FOR.

say and the things you do, your conscience is clear. And, as Ben Franklin noted, "A clear conscience is a continual Christmas." But the reverse is also true. When you engage in things that are out of character, it breaks the peace.

Consistency is to be without hypocrisy, without

duplicity, and without deception. It's a remarkably simple and straightforward way to conduct oneself, and it is, in truth, the only decent way to live.

A man's consistency is what gives a woman security. When he's consistent, she feels confident; when he's inconsistent, she begins to worry because she's not sure what he'll do next.

As I tell men all the time, we're under observation. Our women observe us carefully, cautiously, and continuously.

> A MAN'S CONSISTENCY IS WHAT GIVES A WOMAN SECURITY. WHEN HE'S CONSISTENT, SHE FEELS CONFIDENT; WHEN HE'S INCONSISTENT, SHE BEGINS TO WORRY BECAUSE SHE'S NOT SURE WHAT HE'LL DO NEXT.

So men, please remember this: your woman knows your patterns of behavior, your patterns of language, and your patterns of decision making. Whenever you break any one of those patterns, you can be sure of two things: first, your woman has already noticed. And second, she wants to know why.

Women don't expect their men to be perfect, but they do expect—and deserve—their men to be consistent. Of course, women would prefer that their men also be mature, decisive, and strong *all the time*. Not *some* of the time, not *much* of the time, not *most* of the time.

> WOMEN DON'T EXPECT THEIR MEN TO BE PERFECT, BUT THEY DO EXPECT—AND DESERVE—THEIR MEN TO BE CONSISTENT.

Women prefer men who are mature, decisive, and strong all day long, seven days a week, 365 days a year.

But women are wise enough to understand that perfection is impossibility in this world. So women try their best to overlook *occasional* inconsistencies in their men. It's called forgiveness, and it's an essential part of every marriage. Which brings me to yet another principle that's rooted firmly in human nature: forgiveness works best when it's not needed on a regular basis.

It's easier for a woman to forgive her man once

a year than to forgive him once a week. And it's easier to forgive him once a week than to

> FORGIVENESS WORKS BEST
> WHEN IT'S NOT NEEDED
> ON A REGULAR BASIS.

forgive him *every day* of the week. So problems arise when men behave in ways that require regularly scheduled forgiveness, dished out on an almost-daily basis from the women who love them.

When husbands are *consistently* inconsistent, they abuse the privilege of forgiveness. By doing so, they gradually transform their wives from helpmates to enablers.

Husbands who make a habit of saying one thing and doing another cause their wives to worry. When men proclaim the virtues of godliness but display the values of worldliness, they undermine the foundation of trust that supports their marriage. Thus begins a destructive cycle.

* The man behaves responsibly *some* of the time (and talks up his good behavior).

- But the man misbehaves often enough for the woman to observe patterns of inconsistency.

- So the woman becomes suspicious (with good cause).

- Soon, the man then becomes resentful (because he's managed to convince himself that he's a good man who occasionally behaves badly, not vice versa).

- Then as the man becomes more resentful (and less repentant), the wife becomes more incensed (and less willing to forgive).

For the marriage to last, this cycle must be broken. To break the cycle, the man must acquire the habit of behaving in a consistent manner that's pleasing to his wife, to himself, and to his Maker.

Mature women want their men to act like mature men who are constantly solving problems, not like boys who are constantly causing problems. But the world encourages men to behave otherwise.

The world is continually sending out subtle messages that men can be both mature (when circumstances demand it) and immature (when they want to "chill," or to "hang out," or to "let off some steam"). The world tells men that they can make quality decisions most of the time (when the powers that be are watching) and get away with poor decisions the rest of the time (when the powers that be are looking the other way). The world tries to convince men that "What happens in Vegas stays in Vegas," which means men can behave one way at home and another way when nobody's watching.

These messages, constantly generated by modern-day media, are totally untrue because they violate one of God's basic principles: we reap what we sow.

When we plant good seeds in fertile soil, good things

happen. When we labor in the fields, God rewards us with a bountiful harvest. When we become "doers of the word, not merely hearers," we can expect God's blessings because good behavior, when practiced consistently, brings forth a bountiful crop. It's a principle that applied to Adam, and to Eve, and to you, and to me.

But the flip side of that principle is also true: bad behavior yields a bitter harvest. Proverbs teaches us that, "He who sows wickedness reaps trouble" (22:8 NIV). This principle means that whatever happens in Vegas *doesn't* stay in Vegas, no matter what the casino ads claim.

In life, there are no permanent secrets, only the ones we imagine. God promised that, "Whatever you have said in the dark will be heard in the light, and what you have whispered behind closed doors will be shouted from the housetops for all to hear" (Luke 12:3 NLT).

God didn't say that sinful behavior bears bad fruit *some* of the time. He said we reap what we sow, *all* the time, period. That means that we can't sow bad seeds anywhere on the planet and expect to reap a healthy harvest back home. The world simply doesn't work that way, which is why all of us, men and women alike, should strive for consistency.

CONSISTENT CHOICES

Our lives are filled with one decision after another. Every decision is, quite literally, a personal crossroad, a place where we are free to choose a positive path or a negative one. So in a very real sense, our lives are composed of our choices.

Our choices determine our destinies.

Our actions *today* determine our results *tomorrow*.

Each decision makes its own mark upon eternity, for better or for worse.

So what does all this mean to you? It means that, just as surely as night follows day, *your* choices will determine *your* destiny. If you consistently make wise choices, you'll be rewarded, both in the precious present and in the eternal future. That's the good news. But with the potential for great reward comes great responsibility. And that's either good news or bad news, depending on the quality and consistency of your choices.

If you choose wisely, you'll earn a very bright future; if you choose poorly, you'll construct a very different destiny. But there's one thing you can't do: you cannot *not* choose. Even the decision *not* to decide is, in truth, a decision.

Procrastination is a choice and often a very poor one. When we put off doing the things that need to be done *now*, we tell ourselves that we'll do the right thing *eventually*. But as Abraham Lincoln correctly observed, "You can't escape the responsibility of tomorrow by evading it today."

So the bottom line is this: It's your life, composed of *your* choices, communicated to others by *your* words and *your* actions. And your choices have consequences as well as benefits.

When the devil tempts you, he shows you only the

benefits, never the consequences. He shows you the short-term rewards, not the long-term costs. Satan wants you to make impulsive decisions *right now*, before you take time to assess the potential outcomes. He wants you to make poor choices *today* because he knows that you'll experience serious setbacks *tomorrow*. The devil tries, as best he can, to hide the negative consequences of negative behavior for a very simple reason: Satan wants you to become his servant.

Which brings me to another principle I hope you'll never forget: in life, you'll inevitably become the servant of the choices you make.

That's why you must be careful to make choices that you don't

> IN LIFE, YOU'LL INEVITABLY BECOME THE SERVANT OF THE CHOICES YOU MAKE.

mind serving. And you must make those choices consistently, day after day, one day building upon the next, until the act of making good decisions becomes a habit.

The American educator Frances E. Willard, whose statue is on display in the National Statuary Hall in the

US Capitol Building, observed, "Sow an action, you reap a habit; sow a habit, you reap a character; sow a character, you reap a destiny." Ms. Willard understood that the habits we make today have the potential to become our masters tomorrow. So we must choose our actions carefully, never experimenting with things that we wouldn't want to become permanent features on our personal landscapes.

Regarding habits, Samuel Johnson issued this commonsense warning: "The chains of habit are too weak to be felt until they are too strong to be broken." Thus, every negative habit has the potential to enslave you and, in time, to destroy you. The only sure way to avoid a life-threatening addiction is never to give it a try in the first place.

To be sure that your character and your habits are pleasing to God, you need to make wise choices consistently and confidently. To accomplish this, you must rely on a set of values and principles to guide your decision-making process. Principles accumulate over time as you learn them, as you observe life, as you read The Scriptures, and as you experience the inevitable ups and downs

> TO MAKE WISE CHOICES CONSISTENTLY AND CONFIDENTLY, YOU MUST RELY ON A SET OF VALUES AND PRINCIPLES TO GUIDE YOUR DECISION-MAKING PROCESS.

of everyday living. The Book of Proverbs is chockful of principles; it's an invaluable source of wisdom. But please don't read Proverbs one time and expect to become an instant expert on every aspect of the human condition. The acquisition of wisdom takes time. We learn good judgment gradually—through reading and study, through reflection and meditation, through observation of the world around us and the world within us: our words, thoughts, motives, actions, and attitudes.

The principles that matter most in your life are *not* the ones you proclaim; they're the ones you apply *consistently*. The values that matter most are *not* the values you talk about; they're the values you live by. What matters is constancy of purpose, steadiness, stability, and consistent decision making.

When your deeds match your words—day in, day out—the world knows what you stand for. And your spouse knows what you stand for. Just as important, *you* know what you stand for. When your deeds match your words, you experience the luxury of a clear conscience, but that's not all. You also experience the peace that accrues to those who never need to worry about "covering their tracks," because their tracks never need covering.

When *mature* husbands make *decisive* choices on a *consistent* basis, their wives learn to trust them, and the entire family benefits.

So if you're a husband who's intent on leaving a positive, lasting legacy, you must decide, once and for all, to be the same kind of man *in private* that you'd be proud for anybody to see *in public*. You must become the kind of man you'd want your sons to imitate. You must do whatever it takes to be

> WHEN *MATURE* HUSBANDS MAKE *DECISIVE* CHOICES ON A *CONSISTENT* BASIS, THEIR WIVES LEARN TO TRUST THEM, AND THE ENTIRE FAMILY BENEFITS.

a thoughtful, helpful, responsible man all day, every day, not just on Sundays, or during working hours, or when the family is watching.

God has already given you all the tools you need to be consistently mature, consistently strong, consistently responsible, and consistently righteous. Now He's waiting patiently to see how you'll use the tools you've been given.

Please don't let Him down.

— QUESTIONS FOR REFLECTION —

MEN: If you have the traits of maturity and decisiveness, but lack consistency, what will result? Can you think of a time when your partner was upset by what she perceived as a lack of consistency? How did you handle it?

WOMEN: When your partner shows consistency, how does it make you feel? Take time to praise your partner when his consistent behavior makes you feel cherished.

_____

_____

_____

_____

_____

_____

_____

TRAIT #3: CONSISTENCY

_____

_____

_____

_____

_____

_____

_____

_____

_____

_____

_____

_____

_____

_____

_____

_____

— PRAYERS —

MEN: God, I want your principles to govern my actions so consistently that my wife will feel I'm ultimately trustworthy. Help me spot the inconsistencies and the pitfalls and avoid them by your strength. In your name, Amen.

WOMEN: Thank you, God, for the ways you've uniquely fashioned my husband and me. I praise you for your endless creativity and goodness. In your name, Amen.

— 7 —

STRENGTH

Self-discipline is an acquired asset.

—Duke Ellington

Since the dawn of humanity, women have wanted their men to be strong. In ancient times, women needed their men to be *physically* strong to provide for the family and protect them from harm. Women whose husbands were physically weak were at a distinct disadvantage. In some parts of the world—predominantly in third world countries—women still need men to serve as security guards. But here in the developed world, the need for physical security has been superseded by the need for emotional security.

Today, women deeply desire strength of *character* more strength of *body*. No longer does Jane need Tarzan. She doesn't care if her man can lasso a lion, grapple with a gorilla, or ride bareback on an elephant like it was a

Shetland pony. Nope, today's Jane doesn't want a circus strongman. She wants somebody she can trust.

So here's a message for men: the kind of strength your woman *really* wants has surprisingly little to do with quality quads, or perfect pecs, or bulging biceps. The kind of strength your woman wants most can't be earned in the gym; it must be earned by the decisions you make and the life you choose to live. In today's world, genuine strength is a matter of integrity, not physicality.

—◇—

Strength—the kind of strength that really matters—is the courage to live out your convictions in spite of what the crowd is doing. It's the willingness to stand up for the things you believe in, even if everybody else in the room believes otherwise. It's the dogged determination to be the kind of person God wants you to be, not the kind of person society encourages you to be. Real strength is the willingness to follow the Man from Galilee, not the crowd.

The Bible teaches us that most people who follow the crowd don't know why they're doing it. In fact, most crowd followers don't give much thought to the direction in which they're headed. Crowd followers mistakenly believe that if "everybody else is doing it," then "it"—whatever "it" happens to be—must be okay. As a result, too many crowd-following folks think they're barreling down the main highway when they're actually bumping headlong down a dead-end street.

The problem with following dead-enders isn't that the crowd is stuck; the problem is that the crowd is very *un*stuck and moving *swiftly* in the *wrong* direction. Pastor Rick Warren got it right when he said, "Those who follow the crowd usually get lost in it." In truth, most crowd followers *are* lost. They may not *feel* lost, they may not *think* they're lost, they may not *act* like they're lost, but they're lost.

So it's no wonder that many men have trouble finding their bearings. The crowd is constantly pulling them in one direction while God is tugging their hearts toward a totally different path. The crowd persuades men that strength has to do with power, or money, or fame, or control. But in God's value system, these things are unimportant. That's why some of heaven's greatest heroes will be people you and I have never heard of. God isn't concerned with fame or fortune, and He's not concerned with the condition of your bank statement. He's concerned with the condition of your heart.

God says that real strength comes from love, kindness, simplicity, and humility.

Because the world's values are diametrically opposed to God's values, men are often caught in the middle, constantly struggling to do the right thing but continuously tempted to do the wrong thing. The result is an excess of confusion and an overabundance of anger.

We need to look no further than the daily headlines to see that anger is a societal problem that seems to be getting worse by the day. Senseless violence is a national epidemic, and the trend lines seem to be turning in the wrong direction.

Far too many men are burdened with the mistaken belief that anger equals strength. They believe that by asserting themselves physically—or by engaging in frequent emotional outbursts—they can somehow prove their manliness. But in God's value system, nothing could be further from the truth. Jesus wasn't a bully; He was a servant. He didn't slay His torturers; He prayed for them. The Son of God didn't call upon His heavenly hosts to defeat those who sought to destroy Him. Instead, He willingly carried His cross to Calvary and endured the unspeakable pain and humiliation of crucifixion.

So here's what God says about strength: a man's

> A MAN'S STRENGTH IS
> DEMONSTRATED BY HIS
> GENTLENESS AND HIS KINDNESS.

strength is demonstrated by his gentleness and his kindness.

And here's a message for guys everywhere: your strength, gentlemen, is not demonstrated by some machismo attitude, or by abusive language, or by physical action or angry outbursts. That's not strength; that's insecurity *masquerading* as strength.

"I grew up in a household with a dad who was prone to angry outbursts and a fragile temper. It's dreadful when you have to walk on eggshells in your own home. My mother could never do enough to please him, and she lived a very sad life striving to. Needless to say, our house was not a home; it was merely shelter without peace."

—JACKIE P.

Think about it: if you're weak and you have to move something, you'll struggle with it. You'll shove it and push it with all your might. You might even get mad at it and kick it. But if you're strong, you treat the thing differently, carefully, gently. Likewise, a man's strength is demonstrated by gentleness and kindness, not anger or aggression.

The way a man treats a thing is an expression of his security, his competence, and his sense of self-worth. If a man feels insecure, he turns to abuse and imposition as a way of asserting himself as a man. But in truth, he's merely asserting that he's a juvenile.

In The Living Bible, Proverbs 19:22 says, "A man's kindness makes him attractive." So fellows, if you want to be attractive in the ways that women really care about, you must remember that *genuine* good looks begin on the inside and work their way out from there.

SELF-CONTROL IS AN EXPRESSION OF LOVE

For a man to possess real strength, he must learn the art of self-control. He must learn when to control his temper and when to hold his tongue. As the French archbishop François Fènelon correctly noted, "If you are to be self-controlled in your speech, you must be self-controlled in your thinking." But the devil has other plans in mind. He wants your thinking to be uncontrolled.

Satan wants you to act impulsively, irrationally, and irresponsibly. He wants you to leap before you look. He wants you consider only the immediate rewards, not the long-term costs. Why? Because the devil knows that his best chance to bring you down is to snare you in an emotional web as your temper flares and your basic instincts get the better of you.

"I've seen so many marriages fail due to adultery. There are many outside influences today. Modern culture is obsessed with celebrity and beauty. To make things even worse, much of society lacks solid morals and values. Too often, society only views marriage as an easily changed 'status.' "

—ALLISON C.

If Satan can put your emotions in high gear and your brain in neutral, he knows that bad things are likely to happen, and soon. So if you don't want the devil to snare you in his trap, you'll need self-control, and lots of it.

"I believe anger has a very strong negative impact on the family. It makes everyone fearful, and they tend to shut down."

—KERRY B.

When Satan arrives with a tempting offer, a strong man says *no* without hesitation or remorse. His refusal to compromise his character isn't just a demonstration of wisdom in action; it's also an expression of love.

The man who possesses self-control can lead his family along the paths of righteousness. He can serve as a valued role model to his children; he can be an emotional anchor for his wife. And he can serve as a powerful example to all who cross his path because he possesses a heightened sensitivity concerning the needs of others. Conversely, the man without self-control becomes desensitized to the needs of his wife and children. And troubles begin to accumulate.

> "It takes strength to acknowledge our anger, and sometimes more strength yet to curb the aggressive urges anger may bring and to channel them into non-violent outlets."
>
> —FRED ROGERS

So what should you do if you simply can't seem to find a way to control your emotions, your actions, or your appetites? There are many ways to approach this problem, but as a first step, I suggest you ask the One who formed you to *trans*form you. With Him, all things are possible, and that includes controlling all human emotions, even yours.

INTEGRITY MATTERS

There are no *little* white lies or dirty *little* secrets. In truth, even small lies can have big consequences, and small secrets can grow up in a hurry. As C. S. Lewis noted, "A little lie is like a little pregnancy—it doesn't take long before everyone knows." That's why integrity matters.

Integrity isn't a sometimes thing. You can't turn it on and off on a whim.

If you're a person of integrity *all the time*, your friends and family will notice. If you're a person of integrity *some of the time*, your friends and family will notice that, too, and they'll interpret your inconsistencies as hypocrisy. That's why integrity matters.

If you're honest with your wife, with your kids, with your extended family, and with your friends, they'll learn to trust you and depend upon you. That's why integrity matters.

> **"When someone is dishonest, my first response is frustration and then sorrow. Finally, I'm sad for that person because he or she hasn't learned how to be a real man or woman."**
>
> —SALLY P.

Pastoral counseling pioneer Wayne Oates observed, "Maintaining your integrity in a world of sham is no small accomplishment." Dr. Oates was born into poverty in rural South Carolina; he never knew his father. As a teenager, Wayne worked in a cotton mill to support his mother and grandmother. Eventually, he worked his way through college, became a teacher, a pastor, and a writer. He even coined the term *workaholic*. Today, the Wayne Oates Institute continues to carry on his legacy. But none of this would have been possible if Wayne Oates hadn't maintained his integrity. He didn't look for shortcuts, and neither should you.

It's not easy to maintain your character in this temptation-filled world, but it's worth it. That's why integrity matters to your spouse, to your kids, and to your Creator. And that's why it should matter *to you*.

— QUESTIONS FOR REFLECTION —

MEN: In what ways do integrity and self-control require strength? When you see a man who lacks these qualities, what do you think of him?

WOMEN: Think of a time when your husband demonstrated integrity. How did that make you feel? How important is it to you that your husband shows restraint and self-control? Why is that?

_____

_____

_____

_____

_____

_____

_____

— PRAYERS —

MEN: Dear God, I want to walk in your ways. As the Psalmist says, "Give me Your strength." In your name, Amen.

WOMEN: Dear God, I'm grateful you've wired men to be different from me. I know you've made me strong and I know your desire is that my husband be a man of a different kind of strength. Please bless us as we grow in you. In Your name, Amen.

— 8 —

ON BEING
A REAL MAN

Real Man—a man who is authentic
and genuine in substance. Therefore
a woman can rely on him.

By now you've discovered the four essential things women want from a man: maturity, decisiveness, consistency, and strength.

Women, when you encounter a man with all four, you'll know he's a Real Man.

THE TRAITS OF A REAL MAN ARE MATURITY, DECISIVENESS, CONSISTENCY, AND STRENGTH.

Real men are *mature*; they don't engage in childish pursuits. They resist the temptation to behave impulsively, yet they refuse to procrastinate. When it's time to plan, they plan; when it's time to communicate, they communicate; when it's time to act, they act. A real man's wife doesn't worry that he's spending his precious resources on things without value.

Real men are *decisive*. They make choices confidently and quickly. A real man's wife doesn't fear his leadership because she knows his decisions are based on principles he acquired through both study and experience.

Real men are also *consistent*. His wife can let her guard down and rest easy, knowing his words and actions are based on values and principles that don't change.

Real men are strong. The wife of a real man woman can look to her man and feel proud that he lives out of the courage and integrity of his principles and values. She doesn't have to worry that he's weak and will waver because he consistently lives in accordance with his convictions, no matter what the crowd says.

A real man brings out the best in people and teaches them how to react to change. It's a fair- and foul-weather job. Almost nobody cares who's in charge until things go wrong. That's when the real men show their mettle. And that's when the very best refuse to give up.

So if you're a man who wants to be the leader of your household and a leader in the community—a real man—here's my advice (and by now, you should know this by heart): be mature, be decisive, be consistent, and be strong. And when tough times come, as they most surely will, hold fast to your principles and listen closely to your conscience.

"In the best marriages, husbands and wives have each other's back. They are very supportive of one another, always cheering the other one on."

—RUTHIE S.

— 9 —

A New Beginning . . . Beginning Today

I have simply tried to do what seemed
best each day, as each day came.

—Abraham Lincoln

You've made it to the last chapter. Congratulations! You've completed the first (and easiest) part of this book: you've read and now understand the traits that make a great husband, a great father, and a great leader.

Now comes the hard part—applying what you've learned to the realities of everyday life.

You see, it's easier to talk about being a good man than it is to be one.

It's easier to read about timeless principles than it is to employ them.

It's easier to comprehend concepts than to turn them into habits.

Big ideas like the ones I've discussed in this book are relatively straightforward, so they're easy to understand.

But weaving those ideas into the fabric of daily life is considerably tougher.

So, men, here's my advice to you: take it one day at a time.

Starting today, do whatever it takes to be mature, decisive, consistent, and strong. Don't worry too much about the mistakes you made yesterday. And don't fret too much about the uncertainties of tomorrow. Just focus on the next twenty-four hours.

If you've been a perpetual teenager, drifting from party to party or job to job, settle down. Starting today.

If you've behaved impulsively in the past, slow yourself down. Starting today.

If you've acquired the unfortunate habit of saying one thing (when people are watching) and doing another (when their backs are turned), try a different strategy—today—and bring a little sanity to your life.

If you've been following the crowd since the Carter administration, start thinking for yourself. Now.

Don't concern yourself with the man you *might become* ten years from now. Concern yourself, instead, with the man you *can be* right now.

When you think about it, just 1,440 minutes on the grand scale of a well-lived life, a single day isn't very much. Just 1,440 minutes. But a single day can change everything.

So make today your new beginning.

Today, promise yourself that you'll acquire the four traits women want most. Don't think of this merely as a gift for the woman in your life. Think of it as a gift to the man in the mirror, too.

Today, focus on values you hold dear and practice the principles you find in God's Word. Speaking of God, I suggest that you ask for His help early and often. And then, when you've spent quality time with your Maker, consider enlisting the help of a mentor, a man whose actions you admire and whose judgment you trust.

Throughout the day, make mental notes about the way the world responds to the new and improved you. Then, when the day is done, take a few moments to consider the benefits of being a mature man, living an authentic life, and following your own conscience—not the crowd. Do you feel a little more peaceful than before? A little less stressed? A little more comfortable with your actions and the consequences of your behavior?

If the answer to these questions is a resounding Yes (and I expect it will be), then I give your new lifestyle another one-day try, and then another, and then another, one day at a time, strengthening positive habits as you grow spiritually and emotionally.

When you do these things, you'll gradually transform yourself and your relationships. And everybody will win.

Especially the man in the mirror.

— ACKNOWLEDGMENTS —

I'm eternally grateful to my wife, Karen, without whose love and support this book could never have been written. The principles and insights in this work are the result of successes and failures in my own marriage. They have been tried and proven over forty-three years!

I'd like to thank James Hester and Marvet Britto for bringing us to Carolyn Reidy at Simon & Schuster, who in turn brought us to the team at Howard Books. The team there has been amazing. Thank you Jonathan Merkh, Ami McConnell, Katie Sandell, Amanda Demastus, Jennifer Smith, and the whole Howard/Simon & Schuster team.

I also wish to thank the women whose quotes I've included throughout this text. Their insights and collective wisdom were informative and inspirational. And I thank the many members of the Christian Cultural Center, whose prayers and support have been the bedrock of our ministry.

I'd like to acknowledge the contributions of Edwin Louis Cole (1922–2002), "the Father of the Christian Men's Movement," whose mentorship I still treasure. His work continues, and his legacy endures.

— ABOUT THE AUTHOR —

Alfonso R. Bernard Sr. is the founder and CEO of the Christian Cultural Center in Brooklyn, New York. He has served as the president of the Council of Churches of the City of New York, representing 1.5 million Protestants, Anglicans, and Orthodox Christians. Recently, Pastor Bernard founded the Christian Community Relations Council (CCRC), a New York–based not-for-profit that serves as a central resource and coordinating body for congregations and community organizations.

Pastor Bernard sat on the NYC Economic Development Corporation Board under New York City mayors Michael Bloomberg and Bill de Blasio. He served on the

NYC School Chancellor's Advisory Cabinet under Joel Klein. He served on Mayor Michael Bloomberg's 2001 Transition Team and Mayor Bill de Blasio's 2014 Transition Team.

Pastor Bernard founded the Cultural Arts Academy Charter School, a comprehensive educational alternative designed to meet the needs of children for the twenty-first century; he and his wife also founded the Brooklyn Preparatory School, specializing in early-childhood education.

He was recognized as one of twenty-five leaders reshaping New York (*Crain's New York Business*, September 2008), the most influential New York clergyman (*New York Daily News*, February 2008), the most influential African American New Yorker (*New York Post*, February 2008), and New York's Most Influential (*New York* magazine, 2006).

Pastor Bernard was honored with a Lifetime Achievement Award by Consulate General of Israel in New

York, in conjunction with the Jewish Community Relations Council and the Jewish National Fund. He has also been personally cited in the Congressional Record.

Pastor Bernard has a Master of Urban Studies and a Master of Divinity from Alliance Theological Seminary. He has been awarded an Honorary Doctorate of Divinity from Wagner College and an honorary Doctor of Divinity degree from Nyack College/Alliance Theological Seminary.

He and his wife, Karen, have been married for more than forty years.